D0553685

A View

FROM AN

Empty Nest

BONNIE BETH SPARRMAN

HARVEST HOUSE PUBLISHERS
EUGENE, OREGON

Cover design by Dugan Design Group

Cover photo © by Sergey Skleznev / Fotolia

Back cover author photo by Christopher Erickson

A View from an Empty Nest
Copyright © 2018 by Bonnie Beth Sparrman
Published by Harvest House Publishers
Eugene, Oregon 97408
www.harvesthousepublishers.com

ISBN 978-0-7369-7389-2 (hardcover)
ISBN 978-0-7369-7390-8 (eBook)

Library of Congress Cataloging-in-Publication Data

Names: Sparrman, Bonnie Beth, author.
Title: A view from an empty nest : surprising, poignant, wonderful things on
    the horizon / Bonnie Sparrman.
Description: Eugene : Harvest House Publishers, 2018. | Series: Just for mom devotions
Identifiers: LCCN 2017061161 (print) | LCCN 2018007817 (ebook) | ISBN
    9780736973908 (ebook) | ISBN 9780736973892 (hardback)
Subjects: LCSH: Empty nesters—Prayers and devotions. | Mothers—Prayers and
    devotions. | BISAC: RELIGION / Christian Life / Women's Issues. | RELIGION
    / Christian Life / Family.
Classification: LCC BV4847 (ebook) | LCC BV4847 .S68 2018 (print) | DDC
    242/.6431—dc23
LC record available at https://lccn.loc.gov/2017061161

Printed in China

18 19 20 21 22 23 24 25 26 / RDS-SK / 10 9 8 7 6 5 4 3 2 1

For Eric Paul Sparrman

My love, with whom the nest began,
and with whom it remains secure.

Three things will last forever—faith, hope, and love—and the greatest of these is love.

1 CORINTHIANS 13:13 NLT

Acknowledgments

First and most importantly, I am grateful to God for trusting me with children to love, raise, and release. Additionally, I owe enormous thanks to Eric, my loving husband, who gave me this good life as a wife and a mother and keeps me grounded. I am also grateful to our parents, Elaine and Bendt Bladel and Paul and Gunnie Sparrman, who selflessly let their children go so we could grow up together. They instilled confidence by allowing us to develop our own life and by not clinging too much.

Our children—Johanna (and husband, Dustin), Bjorn, Karl-Jon, and our bonus daughter, Isabel from Germany—enrich our lives every day. They are the reasons I can claim many miracles in the name of Jesus. They have taught me more lessons of faith than they know, and to a person, make me intensely proud of their loving hearts and the way they instill peace wherever they are.

I owe a great debt of gratitude to Todd Hafer, who asked me to share the stories of my empty nest. Also, sincere thanks to Gene Skinner for his talented editing and encouragement along the way.

Though I write in solitude, I am never alone. I owe a huge thank-you to my sister Randi Sparrman, for sharing her faith and insights with me. I am also deeply grateful for the encouragement and blessing of my sisters Kristen Mesedahl and Julie Bladel, and for dear friends: Shelley Frew, Joy Larson, Jean Bristow, Barbara Swanson, Lora "Gus" Plude, Shelly Olson, Karen Huse, Heidi Gustafson, Sue Beck, Kathie and Lee Glenn, our dear Reynard Drive family, and our core group, a.k.a. the World's Worst Parents. Together we have loved our children and eventually encouraged them to fly. Many thanks to each of you for bolstering my faith. What a privilege and joy to trust that God goes with our children and yet remains with us, replacing emptiness with new adventures.

Contents

1

The Chapter Before the First

Surely I am with you always,
to the very end of the age.

MATTHEW 28:20

Last summer we watched with great interest as a mother purple finch carefully crafted a home for her family in a mass of pussy willows that I had tucked into a birch basket next to our front door. Apparently, she didn't realize that location is the first rule of real estate. Or she did, and chose a place that was protected from wind and rain. What she failed to consider, however, was the number of times people run in and out of our front door on any given day. For a couple of weeks, I cordoned off the front walk and porch, lest anyone bother this devoted mother and her loyal mate. With finches, it's the female who builds the nest, though the male brings building materials to the site. We watched them, incoming with bits of twigs, cedar tips, grasses, moss, and finally mud that attached the nest to the pussy willows and eventually to the wall of our house. Mrs. Finch built her home with gusto and efficiency as her husband flapped about, cheering her on. We admired their perfect nest, just the right size, beautifully rounded and soft inside, lined with fur and fuzz.

What came next was nothing less than thrilling. Mama finch sat firmly in the nest, black eyes darting about, as her helpmate brought her meals. And then came the eggs. She produced one each day for three days in a row. Their perfection and beauty took my breath away, with their lovely shape and gentle shade of aqua with dark speckles. In my opinion they were the epitome of springtime itself.

Occasionally, especially during warm afternoons, Mrs. Finch left the nest to fly between the trees in our garden. I could only imagine how stiff she might feel after sitting on eggs all day and all night. It's what a mother bird is designed to do, but it doesn't mean it's always comfortable, and I was glad to see she allowed herself these little breaks during her confinement.

My husband and I peeked into the nest every morning. We were terribly curious about our porch's wild little inhabitants in the throes of starting a family. A mother bird is a picture of patience and beauty, sitting dutifully on her nest of eggs. For two weeks, she held fast to her maternal post while Mr. Finch stayed close by and kept her well fed.

Fortunately, the windows in our front door allowed us a view of the nest without disturbing the expectant mother. We waited with the couple until one morning a bit of commotion announced the "hatch day" had arrived. Mama finch didn't sit still as usual. Instead she shifted from side to side and stood up to turn around. As she did, we spied a pathetic little bird head, no larger than a raspberry, under her breast. The baby's neck was limp, but its mouth was open wide, waiting for breakfast. On each of the subsequent two days, another egg cracked open, exposing a baby bird, fuzzy, wiggly, and full of life. The nest was so full, we feared the little ones might fall out and drop a considerable distance to the porch floor below. But we had no need to worry; the finches had their domestic life in order. The babies' days vacillated between ruckus mealtimes and long naps, and once in a while Mom and Dad finch stole away for a little while, probably to gather food or, we liked to imagine, to enjoy a much-needed date.

For two weeks, the baby finches opened their mouths to their parents, who tucked little bugs and seeds down their throats. The enthusiastic eaters expanded before our eyes. And much like little children, they rolled around, stepped on each other, and competed for Mom and Dad's attention. It was a delight to watch this family. But for finches, "nest days" pass quickly.

Flying lessons began one sunny morning when the air was clear and cool, and sunshine promised balmier days to come. The eggs were not laid all on the same day, and the baby birds didn't fly on the same day either. I surmised that like children, they took off in the order in which they arrived. One by one, the nestlings bravely flung themselves from the nest, clumsily at first, flying in fits and starts with Mom and Dad nearby. It was exciting to watch each little one find its wings and discover freedom in the air. But I wasn't prepared for what came next.

Somehow, I expected the adolescent birds to return to the nest, at least at night to sleep at home and enjoy a good meal and the protection of their parents. But that's not the pattern for finches. Once our feathered friends took off, that was it. In a few days, all we had left to show for the little family to which we had grown attached was a nest that held broken eggshells, a few feathers, lots of bird droppings, and mud.

As I considered the empty nest, I felt a little let down by the brevity of a bird's gestation and infancy. The finches came, built their home, laid eggs, incubated, hatched, fed, and flew away in just one month's time. I could hardly keep up. As I filled a bucket with soapy water to clean up the mess the birds left behind, I thought how fitting it was to have an empty nest by our front door. As I peered in once again, this time noticing lifeless emptiness, I was reminded of the empty bedrooms in our house. Although our children didn't come and go quite as quickly as the finches, the years of having babies and then preschoolers who soon started school and in no time at all became high schoolers…those years sped along incredibly fast. Our nest filled and our nest emptied, leaving us a bit stunned that anything so big and all-consuming could pass with such speed. Did I sleep through it? Did I pay close enough attention to what was happening in the middle of the roller-coaster ride of raising children? How did *I* wind up with an empty nest?

One evening recently, I told my husband I felt more unprepared for this season of life than any other. Like the finches, we had been enthusiastic to create a home and start a family. The beginning was thrilling as we produced three babies in rather close succession. As parenthood started, everything seemed new and exciting! Of course, at times we felt dog tired and overwhelmed as our little ones filled our car to the max and tumbled with each other on the rug after supper like a pile of puppies.

But God in His wisdom usually gives children to young parents, who have generous reserves of energy. Except perhaps when one has an infant, parents of little kids have enough pep to keep up with the demands of the day. And we do so for years…until eventually the last one leaves home, and there we are, staring at empty coat hooks and vacated bunk beds.

The transition to parenthood was a journey that in its infancy required enormous change for us moms. We adjusted priorities, schedules, our social life, income, career, and even the way we interacted with our spouses. We sacrificed much to mother our children. Being a parent has a way of working strands of selfishness out of us simply because babies and kids have needs that surpass our own. We give and give and give for a couple of decades, and we wake up one day to a very quiet house.

On this hushed day, we are not the same person we were before the babies arrived. Such a tremendous odyssey as raising children couldn't possibly leave us unchanged. The years of mothering try us and teach us many things. Hopefully, every day we grow intellectually and spiritually. Physically, over eighteen or twenty-some-odd years, we have changed as well. It may require a bit more sleep to revive us than when we were twenty-seven. And we may not run as fast as we used to.

Whatever our unique situation as our nests empty, it is my hope that each one of us will realistically consider what is particularly challenging about this new phase of being a mom. Do we flip back and forth, jumping for joy one minute and crying over a deep sense of loss the next? Do we pause long enough to recognize the ache in our heart as grief? Does loneliness follow us? Do worries about kids who have recently flown invade our thoughts? What happens to our identity without our precious offspring in our home?

As we adjust to life without children under our roof, may we do the work of intentionally sorting through the emotions of missing them. Let's be realistic and honest with ourselves about feelings of loss and loneliness. By identifying our feelings during this transition, positive and negative, we can discover newfound freedom as a backdrop for renewed joy and energy.

Let's also remember that we do not empty our nest all by ourselves. God surely was by our side, whether we were aware of it or not, when our homes filled with the clamor and commotion of children. And thank God, He remains with us, holding our hands as these same kiddos venture out into independent lives. I will frequently refer to this piece of Scripture through the pages of this book: "Surely I am with you always, to the very end of the age" (Matthew 28:20).

God *is* with us, giving us strength, comfort, courage, and so much healing love. Because of Him, I've written the following devotions to encourage moms whose children are in launch mode. Each section is based on a piece of Scripture, intended to draw us closer to God's gracious love as we allow our children to fly. In the process, may we give ourselves permission to enjoy life in a grand new phase that allows some freedoms we haven't known for years.

2

One Thing
Leads to Another

Let the morning bring word of your unfailing love,
for I have put my trust in you.
Show me the way I should go,
for to you I entrust my life.

PSALM 143:8

My understanding of God's Word as living and inspired by the Holy Spirit comes clearest when a piece of Scripture surprises me with its directing truth at a specific moment. It guides me forward, the way I remember being steadied by the hand of my grandfather as we crossed a creek, step by shaky step, on a slippery log. This is how it was when Psalm 143:8 worked its way into my thinking at a pivotal point when I was a young mother. This chapter will be longer than those that follow because one thing does lead to another...and each of us who stare at an empty nest must have started with the first thing—becoming a mother.

Motherhood sidles up to each mom in a completely

personal and unique way. For me, seeds of motherhood were planted when I was very young. From the time I was a little girl playing with dolls under our locust tree, I was maternally and domestically wired. Certainly, one doesn't need to cook or bake to be a mother, but these activities fascinated me and caused me to identify with my own mom, who excelled at homemaking.

My parents raised four children—two boys and two girls—of which I am penultimate. They taught each of us kids to work hard and to love the out-of-doors, bike riding, swimming, and good food, including Sunday dinners after church.

In some ways, traditional gender roles ruled our home. It was my dad's garage and my mom's kitchen, though each had capabilities in the other's realm. More than once I heard my mother say, "The way to a man's heart is through his stomach," which I didn't forget when I took off for college with a mixing bowl and a bin of baking ingredients.

I attended North Park College in Chicago, where I studied speech communications during the school year. During the summers, I cooked at a Bible camp. This provided a nice balance of city living broken up by glorious summers on a pristine lake in the Upper Peninsula of Michigan.

At college, I became reacquainted with a boy whom I had met at a youth conference in the Rocky Mountains when I was sixteen. But I didn't want him to think he was the only young man I knew on campus, so I dated other guys, all the while holding his friendship in the highest regard. Eventually he and I decided to risk our comfortable companionship for something more romantic. My mom teased me that all those pies and cookies I had baked in the dorm worked their way from Eric's stomach to his heart. I told her I sincerely hoped he loved me for more than my culinary skills.

Trusting that to be true, Eric and I married the October after my college graduation. Eric was already a year into his seminary studies, which kept us in Chicago for nearly four more years. After discovering we couldn't afford seminary and the speech pathology graduate program I was accepted into, I made a last-minute decision to study nursing at my alma mater. The head of the nursing department assured me it would take only three years at two-thirds time to earn my bachelor of science in nursing, and with scholarships, it was much more affordable than speech pathology at Northwestern University. After all, my mom, mother-in-law, and sister were nurses, and I could see the value of being employable in any small town to which my husband might be called to pastor a church. So I became a nurse by default.

The bonus for us was spending four more years in a vibrant academic community that we loved. We enjoyed city life, Chicago's lakefront, restaurants, and concerts, and we joined our first church as a married couple. Our little upstairs apartment with front and back balconies was the envy of our friends. The elderly gentleman who owned the house lived downstairs and was the perfect landlord. He loved us dearly, fiercely protected our privacy, and was stone deaf. When we came home at two o'clock one morning to find the front door locked, we hated to pound on his window, but he cheerfully let us in, teasing us for carousing so late on a Sunday night. Yes, it had taken extra-long to do laundry at my parents' house in the suburbs. Plus, I was studying for a nursing exam in the medical library at the hospital where my mother worked. Such was the nature of our carousing.

While those years weren't trouble-free, they were foundational for our marriage. We had loads of fun, but we also knew devastating sadness when my little brother, a wonderful twenty-one-year-old adventurer, died in a hiking accident at the Grand Canyon. I mention this because it too relates to the empty nest—that of my parents, who were utterly brokenhearted. I felt helpless to comfort them and completely ill equipped to console my sister, who was with my brother at the canyon.

Our whole family fell into an abyss of grief. Even now, many years later, we are still trying to climb out, struggling to make sense of something so seemingly senseless. My anger at a God who would allow such a tragic end to the beautiful life of a responsible young man sent me into a desert of doubt. My brother planned to serve God as a missionary bush pilot in Alaska. At nineteen he had earned his license to fly, and he studied airplane mechanics as a college student. He was hiking for fun on spring break when his life abruptly ended.

I saw my parents' freshly emptied nest in a new light. It was a broken nest, a nest ravaged by unthinkable sadness. I don't know how I managed to complete that semester of med-surgical nursing except by the grace of God. Thankfully, I had incredibly kind and loving professors and dear friends who patiently offered solace. Plus, my husband, who was a close friend of my brother, was a rock for me.

Upon graduation, Eric and I moved four hours north along the eastern shore of Lake Michigan to Muskegon, where I got my feet wet at our local hospital and my husband began work as an associate pastor at a vibrant church. I worked nights for a while because this was required for the job I really wanted, that of a visiting nurse. Eventually, as a nurse on the road, I learned my way around Muskegon County, seeing patients out on farms and in an urban section of the city where our boss recommended police escorts into the high-rises. I put many miles on our little Datsun 310 GX in all kinds of snowstorms, which Michiganders call "lake effect." Up and down the county roads I drove, stopping at my patients' homes to bandage wounds, draw blood, or monitor progress following surgery. Sometimes a patient's greatest need was simply a listening ear, a warm smile, and a hug. I loved the old folks who couldn't wait to see me, but my favorite visits were to pregnant or newly delivered moms. It was through them that I felt drawn to the maternity side of nursing.

My job was diverse and interesting, and I loved the autonomy. Some days, however, dangers couldn't be avoided. Two times snow-covered icy roads sent me into a ditch. Once, when I was bulging at eight months pregnant, the gully that swallowed my car was rather deep, and the guy who towed me back up to the road looked at me as if I were crazy. But I continued to work until our baby arrived, after which I dropped my hours to part time.

The first baby to grace our nest was Johanna Beth, who arrived in March on a springlike day. Moments after the birth, incredible joy and unnerving terror clinched my heart. In awe, I held her wet, wriggling body close to mine and shed tears of joy for us…and tears of sadness for my parents, as I felt more keenly the loss of their son three years prior.

The first six weeks as a new mother present a steep learning curve for each of us, and I was no exception. Being responsible for the well-being of a baby 24/7 is a lot different from caring for infants at the hospital. Like most new parents, we dealt with nights of interrupted sleep that led to exhaustion. When a helpless little one joins the family, many adjustments are necessary. When a baby screams most of the night with an earache, the challenges seem mountainous, but now in retrospect, they seem almost sweet. The three of us figured out life together. Breastfeeding, traveling with a baby, watching for developmental milestones…motherhood (parenthood!) was a strange new world we muddled through, hoping to not make too many errors with horribly lasting effects.

Don't get me wrong; I loved being a new mother. In fact, I wanted to spend all my time with our little Johanna. Taking her with me on errands to the farmers' market or the grocery store made these trips less succinct than they had been, but she was a joy. With a baby in my arms, everyone seemed friendlier. It was easy to talk with strangers who became acquaintances and sometimes friends.

Life in our 1912 bungalow was good. We enjoyed hosting dinner parties and regular church youth group gatherings. On Tuesday nights our living room filled up with students who were eager to hold the baby. We had no shortage of wonderful babysitters, which was a tremendous help.

When Johanna was nine months old, she emphatically decided she'd had enough of breast feeding and pushed me away. It was as if someone flipped a switch. I was dumbfounded. What I didn't realize is that mother's milk doesn't taste the same if she is pregnant. Gulp! That (and morning sickness) confirmed we were expecting baby number two. We began to make plans to renovate the upstairs of our little house. But God had other ideas.

Eric was recommended to become the solo pastor of a small congregation just outside of Washington, DC, in Virginia. I'll admit up front—I don't move easily. I was very happy with our home, our friends, the church, and my work as a childbirth instructor at the hospital where I started my nursing career. Western Michigan felt like home to me, since I had spent every summer of my childhood at my grandparents' house in the Lake Michigan dunes. I didn't want to go anywhere. Moving to Virginia, where we didn't know anyone, at eight months pregnant, seemed insane. But we did it, hoping we were discerning God's will correctly.

Landing in northern Virginia in the heat of August, pregnant with my watermelon of a baby, was certainly not assurance that we had done the right thing. Our new church had a parsonage, which we moved into four weeks before my due date. Our congregation warmly welcomed us, which, in my misery, I thought was the least they could do after insisting they couldn't wait for their new pastor just a few more weeks to give me time to deliver with my trusted physician.

Instead, with a toddler in tow, we scrambled to find a new doctor and a new hospital in thick DC traffic under subtropical sun and humidity. It was a long way from the gentle breezes off Lake Michigan that cooled us all summer long in Muskegon.

At the end of August, my husband's parents drove down from Massachusetts to help us settle and to meet their new grandchild. Their visit must have been a great letdown, however, because each morning they looked disappointed when I showed no signs of labor. We peeled wallpaper and took a few outings, and they played with Johanna while I continued to unpack. A whole week went by, and no baby came before it was time for them to return home. I felt bad, sort of responsible for not producing a baby in time, but despite vigorous walks and even bike rides, baby number two wasn't ready.

Finally, a week later, Bjorn Eric arrived with a thick mop top that made us laugh. He was a big, healthy boy, and Johanna wanted to hold him and make him play with her. More disappointment in the house, but we promised he would grow into a playmate in due time. And while Bjorn was late for one set of grandparents, he was right on time to meet my mother, whose flight from Chicago arrived ten minutes after his birth. She came directly to the hospital, where she was flabbergasted to discover that my nurse had been a longtime work colleague of hers in the hospital where she still worked near Chicago.

I thought, "Really, God, You have an incredible sense of humor!" Between that unexpected reunion and my mom holding baby Bjorn, my heart brimmed with emotion that comes when I see God in the details of life—especially when I think our situation is off-the-charts ridiculous. Our nest was filling, and though we were in foreign territory, God was with us, encouraging our hearts and pulling us along toward greater faith in Him.

We felt like strangers on our new street, but with little ones in the house, we weren't lonely for long. Some of the greatest gifts ever were neighbors who moved in next door and across the street at almost the same time we arrived. Our children were similar ages, and suddenly we had a community right on our doorstep. In addition to our fabulous neighbors, I met a couple of women who were heaven sent. We connected quickly and talked deeply from the get-go. Our children played together while we drank coffee and got acquainted. This helped tremendously.

No matter what stage in life we find ourselves, connecting and belonging with others is key. It's how we feel rooted. I understand myself much better in relationship. This has always been true for me, but my perception of this reality became crystal clear during this season of squirming babies. On one hand, I was never alone, but the babies with whom I spent my time were needy little buggers who required loads of energy-zapping care. Therefore, the other moms around me were lifelines of friendship encouraging survival when exhaustion set in.

But perhaps I wasn't weary enough. By the time Bjorn was nine months old, my breast milk tasted funny once again, and he gave me the heave-ho, hinting what the pregnancy test confirmed by turning pink. Baby number three was in the oven. Our Catholic friends across the street teased us for having more children than they had, and we rounded up one more car seat to stuff into the back of our Volkswagen. It was hilarious to realize we would have three children in three years and three weeks. At least this time we were not moving and I knew my way around the OB department of the hospital where I now worked.

Karl Jonathan, our biggest baby, was a perfect thirdborn who knew from the start it was best to go with the flow. What a blessing, since my husband and I were outnumbered by wee ones. As in each chapter of life, we knew struggles and wonderful blessings. During the baby-toddler years, our friends became the community that filled us up in the absence of our own families. With neighbors we shared holidays, block parties, chicken pox, recipes, delivered meals, family traditions, and afternoons at our neighborhood pool. We prayed for each other and sometimes stepped on each other's toes, but at the end of the day, we were bound together in warm and trusting friendship. We were like a bunch of birds nesting in one tree. Birds who got along and helped one another in all kinds of predicaments.

We shared rides to preschool and soccer practices. Some of the dads coached together, and we cheered from the sidelines with gusto. First days of school took us to the kindergarten bus for tearful goodbyes. We formed school walking groups that kept the children safe and the moms less worried. The rate at which our collective kids grew amazed us, and as a group of ten or twelve parents, we did our best to keep up.

During these years, Eric decided to pursue a doctor of ministry degree. I was all for it, even though we had a lot going on at our house and at church. But he managed to stretch it out for some years so we could maintain sanity. Before he finished, however, God seemed to indicate that we were supposed to move (again!), this time to a developing area just west of Kansas City. But rather than going to an established church, our denomination was asking us to plant a brand-new church. I was devastated.

That summer, while on vacation with my family, God set me down on the sand dunes overlooking Lake Michigan early one morning before the rest of the crew was conscious. He talked to me about this crazy idea of church planting in Kansas. I told Him I didn't want to leave our beloved neighborhood and the friendships it held. I reminded God that our children had a great school and I didn't like tornados. I cried out to God and I reminded Him that moving was not for me. I had moved as a kid and as a pregnant mother, and I had had enough. Next, I opened my Bible and read, "Let the morning bring me word of your unfailing love, for I have put my trust in you. Show me the way I should go, for to you I entrust my life" (Psalm 143:8).

I sat with those words for a long time as the wind rushed over the big lake, stirring the surf and stirring my heart. I did not quickly relinquish my wishes. But I did sense God's presence in the wind and the waves, reminding me that all aspects of my life are His and He would go with us to yet another new place. He massaged my heart with His great love and eased my thinking to consider His call to Kansas City.

At the end of August, we cried with our friends as the moving truck filled, and we took our leave. With heavy hearts, we pulled out of our beautiful neighborhood. I wasn't sad only for myself this time; I felt terrible for our kindergartener, first grader, and third grader in the backseat, whose new school on a Kansas highway would seem pathetic compared to the fabulous school in our Virginia neighborhood. Through tears we saw our friends at the end of our driveway waving us off. It was my husband's birthday, and no one felt like celebrating, least of all myself.

This may seem like a lot of history, but a point I wish to make is that the nest, the home each of us creates, is mobile. With our belongings packed into a moving van and only a temporary apartment waiting for us in Kansas, our car held the essence of our nest. Home was where we were together, and for a few months during the transition, we would hang close to one another in a lousy apartment just off Interstate 35, helping each other adjust.

During painful transitions, I'm never sure how much of my sadness to let the children see. Is it a disservice to share my grief—my *anger* at being uprooted? Or do I hurt them if I try to hide my emotions? I suppose they sensed how I felt anyway. It's something I wrestled with. Attempting to remain open and truthful, but not wanting to bowl little kids over with my sadness over moving, kept me guessing. In relocation there is excitement too, which I am more enthusiastic to share, hoping to instill a sense of adventure for everyone in the family.

As it turned out, we were met by an awesome Kansas City couple, Kathie and Lee, who showed us around and made us feel welcome. While I died of embarrassment, they were amused by our exhausted little children who openly displayed their negative opinion about moving. The children were on their worst behavior, thinking they could perhaps change the mind of those who called my husband to a new job. Our daughter refused to eat anything but pickles and root beer at a Kansas City BBQ landmark, and the boys broke out in a fist-fight during a driving tour of the church plant area. We look back and laugh about this with Kathie and Lee, who in time became extremely special friends for our naughty children.

So while we didn't expect it, Shawnee, Kansas, became the

place where our children did most of their growing up. Our church was established and grew. Our kids made lots of new friends, and so did we—some through church, some through the schools, and some through my work. It didn't happen overnight, but thirteen years was plenty of time to put down roots and collect loads of warm memories with new friends who became our Kansas City family. Our move from the East Coast to the plains was painful, but our nest held together despite the unsettling trauma of starting over once again.

I imagine, in America today, most of us experience this moveable nest in one way or another due to occupations that require relocation. Whether we are the ones with the truck in our driveway or the ones hosting the farewell party, transience touches each of us on some level. My story is not unique, nor were our moves nearly as frequent or taxing as our friends' who were serving in the military or fast-tracking in business. Still, for us, to uproot and reroot was a source of pain and growth.

Through the moving process, I've learned that any location where we create a home-nest can hold meaningful memories that are the backdrop for our collective life. Like our finches in their haven of twigs and fuzz and fur, we grow together under our roof, and as it turns out, the *place* itself isn't the most important thing. Sure, we might prefer one part of the country over another, but truly it's what happens in our homes and in our communities that matters. It's the people with whom we weave the fabric of our lives who anchor us. When we are called to leave those we've grown accustomed to—the ones we trust—the weft threads are yanked out of the warp, and we are left with gaping holes.

When children leave home, another kind of leave-taking happens. Again, big holes yawn at us. Pain that is reminiscent of the sting of moving pounces on us parents, sometimes catching us by surprise.

So the nest fills, the nestlings thrive, and eventually the nest empties. In each phase, God comes alongside as part of the family. When we pause and listen, we discover that He urges us along and shows us the way to go, just as He spoke to me at the beach early on that summer morning before the rest of the household was awake.

Our challenge is to continue to trust God and to allow Him to lead us. He brought us to the empty nest, and He will see us through.

3

The Parentals

We know how much God loves us,
and we have put our trust in him.
God is love, and all who live in love live
in God, and God lives in them.

1 JOHN 4:16 NLT

When children leave home, a parent's identity lurches like a suddenly halted train. Years ago, the younger version of ourselves made the radical adjustment to becoming a mom and a dad. *That* was a huge challenge as we learned that our lives were no longer our own. But over time, the role of parenting became the norm, and as the kids grew up, so did we. I got used to being called "Johanna's mom" or "Mom Bonnie," my alias with the kids' friends. Then sometime during the high school years, the kids jokingly called my husband and me the Parentals, as in, "I'll ask my Parentals if I can borrow the car." And we have come to know ourselves as the Parentals. It is our identity, which feels perfectly natural and normal.

The only problem is that one day those same kiddos who helped define our identities by their very existence do exactly what we equipped them to do. They leave! And as much as we see it coming and prepare for it, when that crazy day arrives, we're a little dumbfounded. We stumble around like flabbergasted children who misplaced a precious blankie. Our sense of self feels off-kilter. Sure, we are still parents. We receive an invitation to Parents' Weekend at college, and we certainly receive tuition bills. But it's not the same as having kids drop their shoes and books by the door and plunk down to dinner.

For my husband and me, the dreaded day of departure happened in one traumatic trip to the airport. Our three had put their heads together and concocted a plan to work at the same summer camp after our youngest graduated high school. So we celebrated our final high school commencement and two weeks later drove to the airport with our gangly offspring, their backpacks, duffels, and hiking boots in tow. For a moment the car had a cheery atmosphere: "*Woo-hoo*...we're going on vacation!" The kids were chatty, taking silly selfies and laughing it up in the backseat. But the forty-five-minute ride wasn't long enough for me, and by the time we reached airport security, even the kids were looking a little forlorn.

They knew I wasn't wild about letting them all leave at once, so perhaps they feigned a few glum expressions to share my mood. My heart felt leaden as I hugged each one goodbye. I did my best to smile through my tears when they waved back at us from the other side of security, and within the hour a 737 swallowed them up and carried them far from home. And that was it! My husband took my hand reassuringly as we turned and trudged back through the terminal. I felt as if a huge, heavy door had just swung shut on a tremendously taxing yet gloriously rich chapter of our lives.

It's not that the kids would never come home again; of course they would. But it would never be the same, just as every season of life is different from the one before. Many questions filled my mind, but the bedrock question was, "Who am I now?"

When weighty questions such as this one seize my heart, I need to be reminded of God's love for me, which grounds me more securely than anything else. I read in 1 John 4:16, "We know how much God loves us, and we have put our trust in his love. God is love, and all who live in love live in God, and God lives in them" (NLT). I would start there. God still loves me and cares about the empty feeling in my heart and the listless, lost sense as I struggle to adjust to a new chapter of being a mom. He has carried me this far, so even as lonely moments are yet to come, I will not face them by myself.

God walked out of that airport with me and back into our quiet house that was soon to be sold. Yes, it just so happened that our kids took off at the same time my husband accepted a new job five hundred miles north of our home near Kansas City. This required heavy-duty grieving. It was only through God's love, extended to me over and over by friends old and new, that I survived that sad summer.

God's love! It sounds so simple, but it is so big, I chose to cling to it and find hope in it no matter how hard it was to pack boxes and leave the house that had been home since our youngest started kindergarten.

So despite the changes, my husband and I are still the Parentals, which means I'm still the mom, even if the kids are five states away and we have a new address. God's love is for real. It carries me through difficult seasons of transition, and it remains the bedrock beneath my feet.

4

Six Minus Four Equals Two and Sometimes One

Blessed are those who mourn,
for they will be comforted.

MATTHEW 5:4

They came in a hurry, filling our home with noise, toys, friends, commotion, and more activity than my husband and I knew what to do with. And they left in similar rapid succession. That's what happens when you have three kids in just over three years and pull an exchange student into the mix during high school. During the child-raising years the house takes on the aura of a dormitory, summer camp, library, gymnasium, locker room, and dining hall. And after a bewildering set of months punctuated by nights fretting over applications, deadlines, college orientations, or visits to the local recruiting office…*poof!* They're gone.

For the mom whose ears are tuned to kids showering at six thirty every morning, those first days in a kid-free house make you feel like death has struck. Where is everybody? Sure, it may feel like a luxury to get up and make coffee for yourself and perhaps a spouse without packing kids' lunches or making their cups of java to go, but the quiet is deafening, and the emptiness unsettling. "O God," you might mumble out loud, "how did I get to be this old?" I'm sure my husband has similar thoughts as he drives past the high school on his way to work. Suddenly none of our kids roam that bustling building after many years of them zipping in and out of classrooms and running on the track.

One morning, over my cup of coffee, it hits me. We were six people living in this house. Then we were five and then four, then three and now two. And every time I find myself at home alone, I realize it's just me. I'm the one left, turning on the radio so someone will talk to me as I clean up the kitchen. The mathematics of this smacks me hard, like a two-by-four to the head.

When kids first leave, I avoid their bedrooms, fearful of the feelings I might encounter if I dare enter. But inevitably someone calls home needing that sweater I had encouraged them to take along in the first place, and digging for it leads to sorting out clothes along with bucketloads of gut-wrenching emotions. This ache deep inside...what is it? I have known this gnawing discomfort before. But when? Pausing to consider, it finally dawns on me; it was when my little brother died thirty years ago and grieving became my second college major. But no one has died this time, so why do I feel the tiresome stab in my stomach like some sinister intruder trying to ruin my day?

I am not skillful at handling grief…partly because of its unpredictable and ill-timed nature. One day I can walk into the high school just to say hello to our kids' favorite teachers and all will be well. But on another day, the same sort of visit might leave me stunned by a ridiculous flood of tears that makes me want to escape and call a friend. At moments like these I find it helpful to remember that God is in the business of comforting His people who need it. He knows when our mother-hearts are breaking and need to be soothed.

Jesus says it so simply in His Sermon on the Mount: "Blessed are those who mourn, for they will be comforted" (Matthew 5:4). Blessed is the mom who is mourning the loss of golden days when her children were at home filling the rooms with warmth and light, craziness and noise—young enthusiasm at full tilt. An actual death isn't required to necessitate the work of grief. And it is work—hard work. Remembering Jesus's words of comfort and care is a good place to start. And give yourself time. You didn't adjust to motherhood overnight, and the same is true for letting them go. It won't always feel as painful as it does when they first leave. So please, go easy on yourself, especially during the first shockingly quiet kid-free months. Allow yourself moments to grieve. They are much-needed steps toward healing.

5

Truth That Leads to Joy

She speaks with wisdom,
and faithful instruction is on her tongue.

PROVERBS 31:26

As a high schooler, I loved to spend time with my best friend, Joy. Many Friday nights we hung out at her house, listening to Billy Joel in her bedroom or baking cookies. Joy and I were inseparable chums, sharing a locker at school and a silly secret way of communicating—we ran toward each other and simultaneously leapt into the air, which meant, "I am so glad to see you!" We called this our "mighty jump" because we were mighty good friends.

We also had a penchant for wrapping our friends' homes and gardens in toilet paper. It seemed like harmless fun compared to the antics of our contemporaries, but Joy's mom, whom I affectionately call Aunt Jean, didn't want us to get hauled off to the police station. At least that was her excuse to drive us around so we could lob rolls of toilet paper into the branches of tall trees. We targeted our beloved pastor and friends from youth group, especially the cute boys we admired.

She graciously drove us in the name of safety, but I think Aunt Jean didn't want to miss our adolescent fun. And she was such a blast, we gladly accepted her as our chauffeur.

But silliness aside, Aunt Jean is a woman of wisdom and truth. One day when I was about eighteen, she made an off-hand comment that stuck with me ever after. As her heartfelt statement fell on my young ears, I thought, "I don't understand this right now, but I imagine someday I might."

It happened when Aunt Jean was deep in the season of releasing her children into the wild world, one by one. In their family, the first three were boys. Next came Joy, followed by two more boys. The eldest was a college student who died tragically in an auto accident, leaving his family stunned by grief. The second studied engineering and learned to fly at the Air Force Academy, and the third had recently taken off for the Colorado School of Mines. Aunt Jean keenly felt the mass exodus of her beloved boys, and she was also grieving. She knew only too well that Joy's time at home was running short. It was around this time that she emphatically stated, "I loved my life best when my children were all around me!"

Her words surprised me because I knew she had loads of fun with her husband, Uncle Bill. I had wrongly guessed they were ready for less chaos in the house and looked forward to more opportunities to sail together and travel freely. They had great adventures all by themselves, but for a moment I glimpsed Jean's heart that ached for the days when all the children were together under their roof.

Her comment brought me back a few years in my mind's eye to when her kids were younger. I remembered the eight of them tucked in shoulder to shoulder, eating dinner around their kitchen table. Sometimes the brothers squabbled, and milk spilled as milk will do, but these children minded their manners. They had great respect for their parents, who taught them well. But now I knew that Aunt Jean's heart was heavy with only half of her children still at home.

It wasn't that Aunt Jean moped around or wore her heart on her sleeve. On the contrary, she was the fun-loving mom who drove us to TP houses and to watch fireworks in Grant Park in Chicago. But she was honest. She didn't sweep all sadness out of sight for the sake of us teenagers. Rather, she stated the way she felt. In fact, it was her pragmatic truthfulness that caught the attention of the eighteen-year-old version of me.

Had her comment not rung with such clarity and truth, it would have passed unnoticed as many adult ideas did. But it made sense; she missed the days when the children were all at home. *Hmm.* Wondering what it was like to miss one's kids, I tucked her words into my long-term memory bank, where they sat dormant until a generation later when the teens in our house began to take their leave.

With our daughter recently off to college in another country, bouts of sadness interrupted the happy mayhem of still having two sons in high school. And whether it was valid guilt or not, I felt guilty for feeling sad that our children were leaving, and life was in a transition that felt painful and unsettling.

But then I remembered Aunt Jean's words, spoken many years ago. "I concur!" I said out loud as I resolutely kicked guilt aside and tucked goodies into a care package for our college student. And I not only concurred; in my head I thanked Aunt Jean for being open about her heartache. The words she shared, so simple and true, exemplified wisdom…and years later, they were instructive for me. What made them especially meaningful was their unashamed admission of grief, which sharply contrasted the cheerful attitude that personified Aunt Jean. She could be happy and sad all at once. She showed me that these emotions often reside side by side as we attempt to make sense of life with exiting children.

To this day, I continue to be inspired by her ability to state what is painful and yet laugh, spreading gladness to those around her. I see her joy as the result of an honest spirit and a deep faith, and I attempt to put what she taught me to good use.

6

Compared to What?

*Pay careful attention to your own work, for then
you will get the satisfaction of a job well done, and
you won't need to compare yourself to anyone else.*

GALATIANS 6:4 NLT

Why does it seem to be human nature to compare ourselves with others? And our comparisons don't stop with who we are. What we do, how we do it, and what we have are all held up against others' actions and goods. This unwinnable comparison game is as natural as breathing and begins when we are very young.

At six, our daughter compared her lunch box to those of her classmates and immediately wanted a new one. And I distinctly remember my delight at being named the tallest in my kindergarten class, a position for which I could take no credit. We were lined up by height for class photos, and I led the line because compared to me, no one was taller. So what? All I had was the farthest to fall.

Again, pecking order was painfully driven home in my fourth-grade math class, where the teacher handed tests back to students in the order of grades, from top to bottom. She began with beaming A students, who eagerly took their papers marked "100%" and worked her way down through the Bs and Cs, finally concluding with those who would rather crawl under their desk than extend a hand to receive a paper marked with a giant red D or F. For me this unjust practice was agony to watch, no matter where I fell in the order. If I did well, I felt terrible for those beneath me, and if I did poorly, as was the case when I was new to the school midyear, I felt completely humiliated. I sat shamefaced in silent misery, convinced that I would never understand long division as well as the rest of my class.

And so it begins, the comparison conundrum encouraged by a hierarchy of status that follows us right into adulthood, undermining a person's self-worth. As adults, we have weightier items to compare and cleverer, subtler ways to communicate who measures up and who doesn't. It's easy to look around us and decide whether we hold a candle to neighbors, friends, and coworkers. Everything is up for comparison: pedigree, a person's career, talents, one's home, car, looks, accomplishments, children, vacations, educational level, and on and on. Who hasn't sat at high school commencement and compared their student to the other graduates? We applaud for the entire graduating class, all the while surmising which student will go far and be a shining success. I'll admit it, I have entertained such thoughts, and I know I'm not alone.

During this time of life, when our children are wrapping

up high school and preparing to vamoose, the tendency to compare is heightened, both for students and for us parents. Perhaps it's the nature of this shifting season. Some eighteen-year-olds are heading into the armed forces, some are beginning vocational school, and some have no choice but to find a job. Others are college bound. Stratification becomes painfully obvious. And if college is an option, does our student begin at community college, a state school, a private college...or are they accepted in the Ivy League with scholarships? Once again, more layers of success, and more opportunities to compare.

So we play the comparison game, looking to see if we or our children are on par with those around us. At this point you might ask, why not? Especially if these thoughts remain unspoken. They seem harmless enough.

But the problem with comparing, even internally, is that it is a dead end. No matter where we look, someone always seems more successful than we are, and someone else is less so. When others look superior, I am down on myself, which builds a foundation for feelings of dissatisfaction or even self-loathing. If I think I land on top, I pour gasoline on the flames of my pride. Neither scenario is productive or good. And if it's the actions or grades of my children that I compare to those of their peers, my disapproval of their performance will only injure my communication with them. I may think my words don't reveal a hidden negative opinion of a son or daughter's efforts, but our children are clever at interpreting the meaning behind what we say and the tone with which we speak.

I'm not suggesting we jump for joy at a child who bombs a class or wrecks a semester. And I'm certainly not in favor of patting ourselves on the back in the face of our own personal failures. Rather, I'm encouraging a fresh attempt at quitting the negative, emotionally draining habit of comparing ourselves and our children to see how we measure up against what masquerades in front of us as successful. (Incidentally, what often appears as worldly success is frequently the opposite. When it comes to possessions, many fall into hideous valleys of personal debt as they live beyond what they can responsibly afford.)

So how do we curtail thoughts of comparison that lay us low? As I see it, comparison that leads to discontent has a powerful antidote. It is called gratitude. When we are truly thankful for who God made us to be and who He created our children to be, we are less likely to waste energy juxtaposing ourselves and our kids with others' successes and possessions. When we cry, "Thank you!" we jump off the crazy spinning merry-go-round that makes us dizzy with envy, and we land surefooted in a place where we can live with ourselves and offer our children encouragement rather than condemnation.

Condemnation of self or others robs our joy. It is a relational wet blanket. On the other hand, words of encouragement spoken to a child who is fresh out of the nest go a long way to hearten the soul of one who might need a rallying cheer.

When we are deeply grateful for every blessing we are given, we naturally take our eyes off ourselves and uplift others. This is true as we relate to friends and to our children.

As we do this, we may have the satisfaction of knowing we are doing at least part of the parenting job well.

7

Tearing Out Their Hair!

*Love is patient, love is kind. It does not
envy, it does not boast, it is not proud.*

1 CORINTHIANS 13:4

Two calls buzzed my phone only minutes apart. Both callers were frustrated parents of young adult children who had returned home for undisclosed amounts of time. While their smart kids had been away earning educations that didn't yet promise gainful employment, the parents, who agonized over the empty nest at first, had discovered its honeymoon qualities. And they liked it! But just about the time they felt content in their kid-free home, college graduation signaled a change. Suddenly a new reality dawned on their knowledgeable grads: Living at home is most economical when trying to save money for the next degree that will render them employable above the poverty line.

So there are Mom and Dad, adjusting again, this time to the arrival of young adult children who have tasted freedom and found it delicious. These older-than-college-age kids have, after all, lived away from home and managed their time, laundry, relationships, deadlines, travel arrangements, finances…and if they've ever gotten into a pickle over lost keys or overdraft fees, they have learned to deal with the consequences quietly and out of their parents' view. They have gained some level of confidence on how to survive in this world.

Therefore, at least according to the parents whose distraught voices wailed into my phone, these grown-up children think they can enjoy the privileges of living under Mom and Dad's roof, but the house rules of high school need no longer apply. And if you thought they were smart at eighteen, you haven't met anyone as brilliant as a college graduate in philosophy who is dying to take on Mom and Dad in a debate. Suddenly everything at home is debatable! Why would you drink decaf when real coffee tastes superior? Why would you allow your corner of the earth to be lawn instead of food-producing vegetable gardens? Why don't you keep chickens? Or bees for that matter? And why in heaven's name do parents speak of such mundane, unintellectual topics? It's a conundrum for parents to know what to discuss at the dinner table that won't be construed as idiotic!

And then there's the issue of post-bachelor young adults' hours. For them, the night is just opening up to premium social time when parents are dragging their tired ol' selves up to bed. But not those college grads. Oh no! They are itching to go out with friends and see no reason why Mom needs to know where they are going. After all, Mom had no clue of their whereabouts for the past four years, so why should she now?

So there we are, trying to love the grown-up child-critic who moved back home to let us know how stupid we are. This is not easy, and in some cases, adult children just need the boot. But in other situations, it can be not only workable but also extremely valuable for both generations.

Here is a special opportunity to get to know our children as adults. We may discuss with them and be amazed, not intimidated by what they have learned. We can choose to encourage rather than frustrate. As they wish to be treated as adults, we may have adult conversations that are more honest and straightforward than ever before. When basic house rules need to be revisited and revised, let's take it on as caring equals, not as parents lording authority. Rather than talk, may we listen…listen…listen. And then listen some more. We might be amazed by our kids' insights and ability to make observations about their home and family of origin. Sure, sometimes it is painfully unsettling to hear their point of view, but the good that comes from candid dialogue is invaluable.

But let's be honest—this takes courage. It requires a good deal of patience to share the house again. And sometimes it takes effort to swallow our pride as we hear our children's perspective on being raised by us. Many hilarious memories may tumble out to entertain once again, but others may hurt as kids perhaps remember some scenarios differently than we do.

May we set aside our pride and hear what our children have to say. We don't have to agree with every word, but just as we wish to be heard, may God give us patient ears to hear and a kind heart to love during this new chapter of mothering.

8

Children of God

*See what great love the Father has lavished
on us, that we should be called children
of God! And that is what we are!*

1 John 3:1

Having children of our own provides an extraordinary place from which to consider how God sees us as *His* children. Think about it: What are the essential, repeated messages we as mothers tell our babies, our youngsters, our high schoolers, and eventually our kiddos who leave home?

From the very beginning, our primary assurance is of our unwavering love. This is easy when they are tiny, unspoiled babies with no guile in them. What's not to love when they are pure and innocent, wiggling pink toes that we can't help holding to our lips to kiss? Even when little children have been naughty, perhaps exasperating us and trying our patience, they eventually fall asleep, our frustration melts, and we stroke their foreheads in soothing love. Teenagers too, in the midst of miserable moments, manage to eke unearned love from Mom and Dad simply because they are our children.

What a mom or dad will do for a child, motivated by nothing other than parental love, doesn't always make logical sense. In moments of grave danger, mothers are known to demonstrate unexplainable strength and endurance to protect their young. A mother will walk miles, lift boulders, and dive into freezing water if it means keeping her child from harm. Mothers come equipped with a special cache of adrenaline, a silent reservoir, unconsidered unless it is suddenly needed to protect a child. Like mother bears, we moms naturally pull out our claws if a child of our love is in grave danger.

And what about all the times we tell our children not to be frightened? We remind our kids that they are strong and competent and that they need not be afraid of all kinds of things. We encourage them to not fear failure or competition that is too stiff. We build them up with words of affirmation; we listen to them when they verbalize self-doubt. We cheer for them with hearts overflowing!

Hmm…both of these messages—that our love is constant and that they need not fear—echo the words that Jesus speaks to us, His children. For us, our loving parent is Jesus, whose affection is stronger and even more persevering than the fallible human love we have for our children. But sometimes we need assurance of God's love for us. Especially when perhaps for a time we forget to stand still in the spotlight of His love. Maybe we haven't had regular conversations with God for whatever reason, and it may have slipped our mind how much He cares for each of us.

When it's time for a "come to Jesus" with, ahem, Jesus Himself...let's first think how much we adore our children and want the best for them. We tell our sons and daughters, "Do not fear! Have courage." And God tells us the same! He reminds us to be strong in Him, to know we are loved and forgiven. In Him we are brushed off, cleaned up, unencumbered by sin. We are free to run forth and live in the joy and knowledge of His love.

In this season of our children leaving home, and maybe even more so because they are exiting, my heart bubbles with affection for them, affection that can literally cause my stomach to hurt. The love of parents for children is powerful indeed. This reality expands my view of my heavenly Parent's love for me, shown in Christ's life, death, and resurrection.

In this beautiful new realization of the Father's love, I am grateful to be a mother whose gut aches with love for my children as they leave home. And I am glad to be one of God's children myself, living securely in a love that is incomprehensibly strong.

How amazing that we should be called children of God! And that is what we are!

9

Hoping for a Heart-to-Heart

Draw close to God and God will draw close to you.

JAMES 4:8

Part of the challenge for an empty-nest mom is having children out there, somewhere in the world, who, when they left, took a good chunk of our heart with them. It's just the way it is as we raise children and let them go. Similar to the way a mother never forgets to feed a baby, once our kids have flown from home, we don't stop thinking about them. But how often do we communicate our caring thoughts to our children in college, or in the military, or perhaps in a new career? And what words do we use?

If you listen to *Live from Here* (formerly *A Prairie Home Companion*), the radio show from Minnesota Public Radio on Saturday evenings, you are likely familiar with the hilarious vignette of an overbearing mother and a rather detached father having a phone conversation with their son, Duane. The melodramatic and needy mother attempts to manipulate her son, who never fails to disappoint her. She cries and whines for him to give her more attention, and angles to unearth any tidbit about his regrettable love life. It's classic; the harder she pushes, the more he retreats. I laugh at her dysfunctional style of relating, but inwardly I cringe, hoping my words don't come even remotely close to this pathetic woman's when I'm on the phone with our boys.

Sure, this mom cares for her son, but whose feelings matter to her the most? Ostensibly she is concerned for Duane's well-being, but through a thin veil of looking out for him, we see a mother who is entirely self-focused. She misses her son, but clearly *her* feelings about the mother-son relationship are paramount. No doubt this boy couldn't wait to get away from home. Even from a distance he is not free from his mother's histrionic schemes.

How do we best release our children and relate to them, communicating trust but not abandonment? How do we tell them we love them even as we let them go? How do we show concern without smothering? How do we inquire about their day without coming across as nosey? How do we truly care for them and not make *our* needs the center of the conversation?

It is a fine line that looks different for each young adult who leaves home. Some children need guidelines concerning finances, relationships, study habits, and follow-through. Each one gains these skills at various points in the growing-up process, so there's not a "one size fits all" answer, even within a family.

If you receive monosyllabic grunts over the phone in response to questions, perhaps it's time to ask a child how they would like you to communicate with them. It seems fair to mention the things that seem pertinent to you and to ask what they would like to talk about. Laying down communication expectations in person can go a long way in opening the door for productive conversations when they are far from home.

Let's remember that timing is everything. When our son is sitting at the Laundromat, he has all kinds of time to tell us about his week and what's going on in his world as clothes tumble in the machines. But if we are chatty when he is trying to study or hang out with friends, obviously, we need to ask when he will be doing laundry again.

Also, it's best to not be like the mom on *Live from Here*, who takes silences and one-word answers personally. Just because we are up for a long, cozy phone conversation, our distant kids might not be in a good place or headspace to talk.

To deal with our heart that feels troubled during moments of disconnect with distant children, let's take our anxious feelings to God. Yes, it is a struggle to keep handing our children over to our heavenly Father, but this challenge is fertile ground on which to build faith. May we not take offense when kids seem uninterested in keeping in touch. Rather, let's be creative in finding ways to communicate our love without overwhelming them with our need to care.

Do we consider the way God feels when we aren't very talkative with Him? Just as we long to hear from the ones we love,

God desires to hear from us. When our children aren't up for a heart-to-heart conversation, let's have one with our heavenly Father, who pines to listen to His kids. Let us draw close to God, and He will surely draw close to us. Alleluia!

10

A Love-Hate Relationship with Social Media

Finally, brothers and sisters, whatever is true, whatever is noble, whatever is right, whatever is pure, whatever is lovely, whatever is admirable—if anything is excellent or praiseworthy—think about such things. Whatever you have learned or received or heard from me, or seen in me—put it into practice. And the God of peace will be with you.

PHILIPPIANS 4:8-9

It's late in the evening, the important emails are answered, I've checked Webster's Word of the Day; it's time to wind down. This is when I'm tempted to turn to social media for a few moments of entertainment or for a quick catch-up with friends.

As I flip to Instagram or Facebook, it's often to wish someone a happy birthday, to send a personal message, or to touch base with friends with whom I share interests. What is baker Juli putting in her oven this week in the Ukraine? What is blooming in Molly's garden? Have our friends posted photos of their son's wedding that was the highlight of last weekend? Did our children share pictures of their recent apple cider making event? Have my former classmates in Sweden been together lately?

These are worthwhile interests, and it's fun to scroll through Instagram or Facebook to instantly enter the world of many whom I care about and love.

But some evenings the scrolling goes on too long, and the list of "friends" extends beyond the definition of the word. I keep trawling for nuggets of social information, almost as if reading *People Magazine* about those I actually know—or at least remember their name and something about them.

It offers some level of relational connectivity, but this type of relating also comes riddled with landmines with the potential to pull me down. Sometimes I'm captivated by another's adorable grandkids or their beautifully set table. And while there is nothing inherently wrong with this, I wonder at the empty feeling that often pervades my soul after I've wasted twenty minutes applying my mental thumbs-up or thumbs-down to many a post. In some instances, I applaud my friends. In others, I share their grief. On some pages I feel disgust, and with others I am moved to compassion and a deep desire to reach out and help.

But sometimes I come face-to-face with envy. I compare the truth of what I know about myself with what I *don't* know about my friend who posts carefully cropped, even retouched, perfect photos. The reality of my life is messy. It includes a house that needs repairs, a garden that has been ignored half the summer, a relationship in tatters. I'm dog tired and need a haircut, and it feels as if all we do any more is work. These personal shambles are what I compare to my "friend"—really an acquaintance from high school, who has just completed her fourth marathon along with her supersuccessful children. They stand by, medals glinting in the sun, smiling with Chiclet teeth at their glamorous mom. Yikes, certainly my shortfalls are magnified when I compare myself to her. Part of me feels fifteen again, awkward and subpar.

Still, I engage in social media. One reason, as empty-nest moms know, is to snoop on our children. It's our surreptitious way to catch a glimpse of our kids' lives—sort of like peeking through a security camera at what they are doing, who they hang with, and what they are concerned about. But even this works better with established boundaries.

If I look at my children's Facebook pages or on their Instagram, I may not like what I see. I might disapprove of their choice of words, and the issues that stir their heart are different from mine. So I must decide, how will I respond to these posts? Am I okay with remaining a silent observer? Or will I talk with my son or daughter about their posts, realizing it could damage our relationship? Am I hovering too much? A young woman recently confided in me that her mother unfriended her over differing political opinions that came to light on Facebook. "Who unfriends their own *daughter*?" she implored with a distraught and broken heart.

We must do better than that! No comment is worth throwing a chasm between ourselves and our children. We may differ, we may feel offended and worried about the ramifications of a polar point of view, but we must love. Part of that means allowing our children the freedom to form their own opinions, to express themselves, and not to be squelched and censored by parents. Sure, we may engage in constructive conversation, but even there, our willingness to listen and ask good questions could be more effective than delivering a lecture.

Millennials and post-millennials who perceive that parents have invaded Facebook and Instagram often move on to other avenues of social media, such as Snapchat, with its disappearing content. Not all, but certainly some revolt from helicopter parents who hover too low and too loud. The children declare independence.

But child-parent relationship aside, how does social media influence my own heart—how I think and how I feel? I realize this is different for everyone, but I'd like to pose a few questions worth considering for empty-nest mothers:

- If I say I don't have enough hours in my day, why would I spend a lot of time on social media?

- Am I filling a void that was previously filled by the presence of children at home?

- Might my emptiness be satisfied in a more constructive way?

- Am I being sucked into the vortex of social media out of loneliness?

- Do I have an overdeveloped need to be "liked"?

As an entire generation of techno-savvy individuals comes of age, researchers explore the effects of social media on the human psyche. Are we surprised to learn that it is possible to be addicted to social media? When we receive a "like" on our Facebook or Instagram post, the pleasure center of our brain receives an emotional rush of satisfaction.[1] It's easy to see how this happens. Many of us innocently join the game without being aware of the potential need to continue playing more, posting and posting, waiting for likes.

I get it. I too like to be "liked." Who doesn't? A few weeks ago, I innocuously kneaded a lump of cardamom bread dough. It just happened to be an extra silky, springy batch, caused by the mysterious combination of perfect weather and ingredients that got on well together, under ideal conditions beyond my control. My daughter sat across the counter from me, mesmerized by the rhythmic turning and pressing of the dough. I said, "Isa, video this for me, okay?"

She picked up my phone and caught thirty-five seconds of my hands manipulating dough, which I uploaded to Instagram. My number of follows doubled that day, and I felt good about my bread and the response of those who joined us in the kitchen, if only virtually.

It isn't wrong that my heart is warmed by friends who

comment kindly that they would like to join us to make bread. And I'd welcome this bunch of baking enthusiasts to come and bake and drink coffee and taste the spoils. But I also see how addictive these affirming responses are. Every time another little red heart lights up my phone, the pleasure center of my brain tells me I'm doing okay, at least for the moment. But woe to me if I *need* to elicit these cheers from afar. Living to be liked is dangerous.

Another question about my interaction with social media begs to be asked: Does my husband love me more if he expresses his anniversary wishes to me for the world to read, rather than keeping his words of endearment between us? Do we need five hundred friends to approve our special day? In the same vein, need I tell my children how much I care for them via social media? I ask rhetorically, knowing that love within our family is not hinged on cyber comments. But it is a question worth pondering.

One more aspect of social media worth considering is its influence on relationships. Do we allow social media to take the place of interpersonal communication with our family members and closest friends when plain old conversation would be more constructive? In other words, do I *talk* with my siblings rather than expect them to know what is going on in my life by assuming they read my Facebook page? Nothing takes the place of person-to-person conversation, especially within families.[2]

During Lent, that special season of introspection and extra

focus on Christ from Ash Wednesday to Easter, I give up Facebook. Each year, I miss it at first, but as the weeks go along, I discover greater calm and a growing peace in my soul. A certain tension is gone. Part of me misses my cyber community, but then again, how natural is it to remain friends with every person I've known from every decade of my life and from every place I've ever lived? It can be exhausting. Once in a while a Facebook interaction leads to deep, worthwhile sharing, but more often than not it is superficial rubbish that leaves me as lonely as I was when I signed on.

Let's return to these profound words from the apostle Paul:

> Finally, brothers and sisters, whatever is true, whatever is noble, whatever is right, whatever is pure, whatever is lovely, whatever is admirable— if anything is excellent or praiseworthy—think about such things. Whatever you have learned or received or heard from me, or seen in me—put it into practice. And the God of peace will be with you (Philippians 4:8-9).

Is my social media communication worthy of this description? True, noble, right, pure, lovely, excellent, praiseworthy?

Late at night, when it's time to tuck myself in, perusing Facebook is not the best way for me to end the day. I find it defeating. For me it is a lot more meaningful to share a face-to-face conversation with my husband. Or if that is not possible, I pull out a piece of stationery and write a real note to a *real* person, perhaps another empty-nest mom who needs encouragement. Or I write a few lines to one of our children who could use a note from Mom. This simple practice drives away loneliness for at least two of us—myself and the person to whom I write.

Or I pick up a good book, another type of companion, and read a few pages that inspire and uplift. Tonight I turn to Madeleine L'Engle's *Irrational Season* and find myself delighted by her setter dog who romps with a sparrow all summer long. The beauty of her descriptions and the truth with which she speaks put my mind at ease as the pillow beckons.[3] I know I have learned, received, and heard from God. I close my eyes, and I find peace.

11

Deliver Us from Envy

A heart at peace gives life to the body,
but envy rots the bones.

PROVERBS 14:30

In the last chapter, we talked about some positive and negative aspects of relating to others with the whole world listening in. Communication on social media is as exposed as a billboard. But the results of this phenomenon are private. What is said out there affects how I feel deep in my soul. And sometimes when I've let Facebook dominate my thinking, I don't feel very good. I'm left to deal with that insidious enemy—envy—when others' lives come across as far superior to mine. And envy, that lousy four-letter fiend, is a robber of contentment.

We all know how it works on Facebook; take twelve selfies of yours truly and a friend doing something uncharacteristically brave or brilliant. Cull through the photos to see which is the most impressive. Upload immediately so 650 of your closest friends won't be denied the chance to applaud your moment of glory. It could be anything—a phenomenal sunset while you stroll on a beach in Tortola, or perhaps your perfectly composed salad complete with orangey-yellow nasturtiums rimming the plate.

I must admit, I enjoy seeing the lovely blooms on my friends' rose bushes, or dishes of pasta and grilled vegetables that look like a page in *Bon Appétit*. And I especially thrill to the faces of babies who mature from one picture to the next. But sometimes the discrepancy between others' exceptional lives and mine causes me to sin.

First of all, I sin in my critical little head because I am repelled by what appears in some cases to be narcissism on display. Selfies, selfies, selfies, announcing validation! Humble-bragging, all too often eliciting the opposite effect it attempts to communicate.

But I'm also duped into believing the pictures that make everyone else's life look charming, beautiful, glitzy, and put-together. I am positive mine can't possibly measure up. It's terribly easy to envy the successes of others.

We see graduation photos, one day of sunshine and glory, and wonder if our children will ever get there. Yes, the college commencement picture is lovely, but what we don't see are the dark hours of doubt, pain, counseling, and medication necessary to bring a student to this outward moment of success. And we don't peer into the agonizingly deep cavern of debt necessary to make this day come to pass.

Along with graduations, the years of the empty nest are replete with weddings in our children's generation. Each one looks more dazzling than the one before, and again it's easy to envy and wonder what a wedding might look like for one of ours.

Even with this head knowledge, I am caught in covetousness…and it is a pack of trouble. I may pray, "O Lord, please deliver me from this inward struggle, where I wonder if You have smiled on my friends more than You have smiled on me." In the shadow of all that goes well for my neighbor, my life is pale gray. I know my own struggles intimately. About my neighbor, I know the outward good looks and the obvious victories. And the more I focus on the discrepancy between their blessings and my trials, the worse my plight looks in my myopic lens.

But why am I using others as my benchmark? What does God say about this spiritual struggle?

For one thing, He says plainly and simply, "You shall not covet your neighbor's house, you shall not covet your neighbor's wife, or his manservant or maidservant, his ox or donkey, or anything that belongs to your neighbor" (Exodus 20:17). In other words, we should not be so sure that another person's situation, spouse, child, or home life is better than ours.

God in His wisdom knows what covetousness does to our spirits. "A heart at peace gives life to the body, but envy rots the bones" (Proverbs 14:30). Our bones! The framework that holds us up, to which our muscles cling so we may be moving, active bodies. No one goes anywhere with rotten bones. When we allow ourselves to be consumed by thoughts of wanting what someone else has, all contentment leaves us. We are wobbly, helpless, and immobile. And we are terribly ungrateful.

So how do we move beyond the tyranny of envy? How are we cured of rotting bones?

As with the need for healing in any part of our lives, we need to recognize places where we've allowed envious thoughts to invade and cause dis-ease. When do I give in to wishing I could be more like someone else, or wanting to have what someone else has been given?

Perhaps engaging in social media does not cause you to stumble as it does me. But research shows that one in three people feel more dissatisfied with the reality of their own lives when they spend time cruising their newsfeed on Facebook.[1]

What would happen if we were to exchange envy for thankfulness? Every time we make a mental comparison that elicits a twinge of pain because we notice we have less, or receive fewer accolades than a friend, or our circumstances have been tough, let's thank God for walking the path with us. It could be that our blessings come through the aches and struggles that are ours.

Am I willing to believe that envy will not get me anywhere? Can I try to unburden myself of its grip? Will I write down everything I feel envious of, anything I covet, and hand it over to God by burning up the list? Yes, with a match. Get rid of it! And in its place, offer thanks.

I don't mean pie-in-the-sky thanking God for difficult struggles that come our way. But *in* the struggles, thanking

God for His graciousness and love. Thanking Him for being available and for caring about us and our children.

Let's be willing to let God heal our aching bones, our tired bones, which grow weary under the weight of envy. Let's walk upright, straight and tall, trusting that thankfulness has the power to wash away envy. This may be a daily struggle, but one that is worthwhile.

12

More Peaceful than a Mud Pit

The LORD is my shepherd, I lack nothing.
He makes me lie down in green pastures,
he leads me beside quiet waters,
he refreshes my soul.
He guides me along right paths
for his name's sake.

PSALM 23:1-3

Today, the view from my empty-nest patio is literally that of a tidy backyard. Though I have not been a diligent gardener this summer, thanks to the previous owners of our house who planted perennials, flowers flourish. Trees that require little care offer shade and a sense of peace, for which I am grateful. In this place we now call home, which is different from where we had our babies, God has truly led me to rest beside quiet waters. Each morning when it is warm enough, I take my coffee outside to enjoy the beauty of nature, which gently restores my soul.

Perhaps this seems especially sweet to me because this has

not always been the condition of our little plot of earth. What a contrast between the tranquility of this present scene and my memories of years past when our yard was a disheveled mud pit. When the kids were small, the center of activity on our corner lot was a pentagon-shaped sandbox that held a dynamic construction site complete with yellow dump truck, backhoe, sand mill, shovels, buckets, and watering can. Every spring we dumped two hundred pounds of fresh beach sand into the box, which we eventually swept from the kitchen floor a quarter cup at a time.

Beyond the sandbox was a tree swing, and sometimes a blow-up pool or makeshift tent. But the greatest gift to our kids was a giant spruce tree under which they established their secret hideout. Beneath thick branches, hidden from sight, was a perfect child-sized room, cool and fragrant, heady with evergreen air. For children, this secluded hideaway was heavenly. Sometimes at bedtime, when a favorite blanket or teddy couldn't be found in the house, I crawled under the tree with a flashlight to locate the precious article required for sleep. It was a task I enjoyed, creeping into the kids' sacred space, smiling at the remains of a tea party or a collection of stones lined up on their "luck log." I remember wanting to stay, to breathe deeply of the sweet spruce, loving the quiet after a hectic day. I wanted to remain and sleep under the spruce, so hungry was my soul for solitude and peace.

The bustling years with three preschoolers left little time for quiet reflection. I longed for it. In fact, when the kids were babies, I made an agreement with God that I'd devote to Him the first five minutes of quiet that might come my way. Just finding five minutes required strategy. It was a trick to arrange preschool pick-up and lunchtime for two kiddos, along with nursing a baby. My best friend, who also had several toddlers, joked that the sun and the moon must align perfectly for naptimes to overlap. If I had five, ten, or fifteen minutes all to myself, I was doing great. That's when I'd flop across our bed or collapse on the couch to read from the Bible. On a good day, I might even have time for a conversation with God in my journal. These minutes were precious and few, but they remain in my memory as vital and life-giving. To survive spiritually, I had to grab whatever moments I could get and make the most of them. It meant ignoring dirty lunch plates smeared with peanut butter, and overlooking crumbs under the table. Similarly, I had to overlook a messy backyard that reflected the condition of my heart.

This is why I am grateful for our empty-nest backyard. I don't want to forget that I have more time to sit beside quiet waters or by a plot of thriving grass, where God refreshes my soul. It is a gift to look out at a garden that is no longer a sea of mud and toys. My husband and I would gladly welcome grandchildren to come and make an inventive mess of our yard once again, but we are not there yet. So in this quiet hiatus between children and potential grandchildren, I am thankful for the way God draws me near and refreshes my soul.

It's not that He wasn't there before; it's just that now He is letting me enjoy a less chaotic place. It is also quieter, which helps me listen for His voice. With great concerns for children who are far away and for our own children who need constant prayer, this gift of soul refreshment is not lost on me. It is a bonus of the empty nest.

When the kids were little, they had plenty of needs, and we had our share of concerns. But many of their needs were met through our actions. So much of our energy went to nurture and care for our babies and small children. But now that our children are young adults, our prayers for them seem more necessary than ever. How clever of God to give us more time to engage in prayer and to grow deeper in faith ourselves in this present season.

He truly does lead us beside quiet waters. He wants to restore and refresh our souls. In His great love for us, He wants to guide us down paths of righteousness, which of course is much more likely to happen when we sit with Him, noticing His presence in the breeze that moves through the trees—and in a so-so garden that is no longer strewn with toys.

13

Keeping the Faith

*Without faith it is impossible to please God, because
anyone who comes to him must believe that he exists
and that he rewards those who earnestly seek him.*

Hebrews 11:6

*I have fought the good fight, I have finished
the race, I have kept the faith.*

2 Timothy 4:7

*If you have faith as small as a mustard seed, you can
say to this mountain, "Move from here to there" and
it will move. Nothing will be impossible for you.*

Matthew 17:20

When I tuck myself into a cozy patio chair early in the morning to watch the sunrise, I know God is leading me beside quiet waters. I cuddle a hot cup of coffee that is kept warm by a linen napkin draped over and around it. Steam rises through the fabric and smells like the pastry cloth on which my mother rolled pie dough years ago. I breathe deeply, thanking God for her and the rest of the family. I eat a little breakfast, read, write, pray, and listen to the birds and other wildlife playing in the trees. But eventually I must unfold my legs, get up, and get busy. I can't spend the entire day hugging my coffee and basking in quiet repose. The sun shifts and breakfast is over. It is time to get to work.

As I see it, sitting still, reading God's Word, consciously drawing near to Him…this is one aspect of developing faith. It supplies spiritual food and is vitally important if we are to grow our relationship with Christ. But another equally valuable way to help expand our faith is to put it into action.

Have you ever prayed for your belief in God to be stronger, more impressive and robust? "O Lord," we say in all earnestness, "please give me a large measure of faith, enough to sink my doubts for good." And we sit back and wait for the faith truck to back up and deliver a fresh load, as if it is loamy topsoil, rich with nutrients.

This makes as much sense as desiring to be good at playing the piano but never sitting down to practice. Or anything else that requires hard work to develop skill. If I want to be a competent swimmer, I'd better jump in the pool and learn how it's done. To dance, we need to master the steps and use them. A lot! Over and over, until we don't have to think where to put our feet. Eventually motor memory takes over, and we're able to move on to the finer points of style and having fun with our partner.

It is similar as we attempt to develop a strong faith in God. Just talking about it doesn't make me a better follower of Jesus.

To have greater faith, I need to act on the bits of belief that are mine.

I used to envy the strong faith of Georgia, my friend's mother, who was one hundred and one years old. She spent a couple of hours each morning praying and reading her Bible. I assumed her faith was tenacious because she was very old, but actually, her faith was strengthened because she prayed so diligently and heard from God through His Word. And she lived her faith. Through all life's challenges (and she knew plenty), Georgia took her concerns to God in prayer. This was her lifestyle. As she grew old, her eyesight failed, but she did not grow bitter or complain. Instead she reviewed the many Bible verses she had memorized when she was young. When she was tempted to worry, she recalled Psalm 56:3, "When I am afraid, I put my trust in you." Between the Scriptures she knew by heart and her near-constant conversation with God, she logged thousands of hours in prayer.

Faith is a funny idea to ponder because, like the wind that stirs the tops of trees or furls the sails of a boat, it is invisible. But we feel it. We hear it. And we see what it does. Similarly, we observe the results of faith in lives like Georgia's.

Because of faith, my friend Jane bravely and honestly grieves the premature passing of her husband. By faith, our longtime friends Barbara and Steve leave our relatively safe and comfortable community to minister to refugees across the ocean, far from their families. And it is faith in God that allows my friend Joan to face death with peace and equanimity even though she will leave behind her loving husband of many decades. It is faith in God that urges us to be stalwart and sometimes to do what we think is impossible.

By faith I will trust that God never takes His eyes off my children. By faith I choose to believe that God will give me the wisdom and strength I need to care for aging parents and young adult children. By faith I will not give up on faith.

Is God calling us empty-nest mothers to grow our faith in Him through bold action? What does that look like for you? For me? Maybe it means not freaking out when a son or daughter calls with news that registers as alarming. When our son recently said he bought a ticket to fly to Hong Kong to sell a piece of art, I wanted to pepper him with questions. "When? For how long? Where will you stay? Are you going alone? How can you afford the ticket? Is this for school or part of your side hustle? How can you take time away from your job at the lab?"

And that's just one little subject with one child. Each mom lives through many versions of this conversation with weightier topics to discuss. We hope our kids will do what is right, what is best, what will be most beneficial in the years to come. We want to have faith in our children, which is often a test of our faith in God.

Still, I maintain, we must do more than just pray for greater faith. We need to *act* on the itty-bitty mustard seed of faith we have. As we trust God to help us take the first step, He leads us to the second. Our goal is to trust God with everything that matters to us, but we begin with one small thing and then add another and another.

When our children were little, I regaled them at bedtime with "Amanda stories." These were made-up tales of three children who were strikingly similar to our three. Each story included a lesson or moral message, intrigue, adventure, and something ridiculous. The children begged for the next installment of Amanda, Harold, and little brother Karl. Mind you, I was an exhausted mother who needed bedtime myself, so making up these stories stretched me beyond what I thought I could compose. But as I started out, one twist in the plot carried us to the next, and by the time I said, "The end," a lesson was conveyed, the children were entertained, and we were all ready for bed. Sometimes I told these stories in my sleep. When the children relayed them back to me the following day, it was as if I had heard them for the first time.

My point is that each piece of the story built on the one before it, sometimes beneath my consciousness. Faith is like that—a journey of one trusting move that brings us to the next. As we act on what we believe, God is faithful and keeps leading us along.

14

Dropping Them Off

*Peace I leave with you; my peace I give you. I
do not give to you as the world gives. Do not let
your hearts be troubled and do not be afraid.*

JOHN 14:27

Releasing children from home to their next adventure in life is part gradual process and part ripping off the Band-Aid. For some moms, the senior year of high school is an exercise in pre-grieving as we sniffle our way through their last sporting events, art shows, and musicals. All too soon the festivities of commencement are upon us. We cling to the best of what high school has been for our child and marvel at how they have matured. For some mothers, however, their student's senioritis is so acute, the desire to fly so caustically communicated, that parents are nearly ecstatic that the kid will soon be packed and gone. I'll venture to guess that most of us vacillate between these antithetical positions, but for each of us, the time will come when our fledgling will fly.

In our family, one autumn of leave-taking was particularly poignant. Thanks to the service of our ancient but trusty minivan, we managed to haul all three kids to college in one momentous trip. The first stop was North Park University in Chicago, where our daughter began her senior year. Bringing Johanna back to happy reunions with friends was a joy. Still, my heart twanged as her brothers, also known as the Tall Trees, reached down to hug their sister goodbye. After their entire summer together, I knew they would miss each other tremendously.

Next we rounded the bottom of Lake Michigan and headed up to Grand Rapids, Michigan, where our boys, a sophomore and a freshman, were assigned to the same dorm at Calvin College. And what a surprise to discover, of all things, that they were given rooms next door to each other. As their mom, I was thrilled, and the boys, being best friends, were delighted as well. They each had a roommate, but they also had a brother next door.

We proceeded to unload their gear from the van—bicycles, duffels, toolboxes, posters, coffeepot, bedding, and bookshelf. The dorm was alive with parents and students toting boxes, arranging rooms, meeting one another, and figuring out how to hang bikes from the ceiling. Somewhere in the process of bunking beds, it became apparent that our freshman had had enough of Mom and Dad's help. After all, being last-born, Karl-Jon spent his senior year of high school sibling-less under our roof, and by now every fiber of his being screamed for independence. So we backed off and made ourselves useful in his older brother's room. Bjorn was only too eager for our assistance in turning stackable furniture into a loft bed that was as tall as his six-foot-six-inch frame. We played with the various pieces of furniture as if with giant Legos, and when we had it the way he wanted, we all went out for pizza.

For me, delivering children to their next place is wrought with awkward moments, trying to sense when I am helping too much, stepping too far into the confines of their new life. Do we drop the duffels and run, or do I get to make the bed one last time? I realize this bed making is probably more comfort for me. I attempt to gauge the needs of each boy—the fiercely independent first-year son, and the second-year son who doesn't seem to mind our presence so much.

After pizza, with one boy ready for us to go, we think it's best we say our final goodbyes. I want to meet for breakfast, but we decide to hit the road early and let the brothers settle on their own. As we hug our farewells, Bjorn, with one year of college under his belt, says, "Karl is so ready for you to leave, but he doesn't know how lonely he will feel in three months." Gut punch to mother! Oh…sweet tall son of mine who admits he misses us when we are far away. I hug his waist, my head not reaching his shoulder, and I cry my love onto his musty T-shirt. And dear Karl-Jon, itching to be on his own, I hug him as well, and he sweetly hugs back, sorry that it hurts me to leave. And then we go.

With my heart in my throat, we head to our hotel. I try to sleep. At least I'm comforted by the fact that Johanna has great friends, even a dear cousin in her campus house, and the

Tall Trees have each other as well as Bjorn's friends from last year. In the morning, we get up early and begin our sad seven-hundred-mile drive back to Kansas, to pack our house and prepare to leave that as well.

An hour outside of Grand Rapids, my phone rings, and I'm delighted to see it's Bjorn. I eagerly answer, "Good morning!"

But all I hear from his end is mumbling and crying. I tell him I can't understand him…he cries harder, mumbles more, and then I make out the words, "…and there's blood everywhere!"

My mind races; my heart stops. "O *God*, what has happened?" I grab Eric's arm and demand an illegal U-turn. I ask Bjorn where Karl-Jon is, who at that moment happens to walk in and take the phone. I practically yell, "Karl, what is going on? What happened to Bjorn?"

Karl-Jon vaguely answers he doesn't know, but Bjorn is on the floor next to his bed, his head has a gash, and the carpet is a mess. I tell him to stem the bleeding and call for help; we will be there as quickly as possible! We speed back to campus, Eric concentrating on the road while I deep-breathe and bite my lip.

"Good grief!" I chew out God in my head, "we leave our precious boys for one night, and something awful has happened. I am terrified! How can I trust You?"

As it turned out, Bjorn rolled out of bed in his sleep, hitting his head on a sharp edge of a bookshelf on the way down. We suspect he passed out because he lay on the floor, half wrapped in his comforter, which along with the carpet had absorbed a lot of blood. He wasn't aware of anything until he was awakened by pain, saw his own blood, and called us. It was a long way from bed to floor.

We spent most of the day in the emergency room getting sutures, a CAT-scan, and an EKG, and cleaning up scrapes on legs and arms. When the doctor realized that alcohol was not involved, he joked with us that of the six colleges nearby, Calvin students are the klutziest.

"Oh goody," I thought, "what else will happen?" My heart was still reeling with fear. Harm can strike our kids at any moment, even when they are innocently tucked into bed for the night! I wasn't comforted by the doctor's lighthearted comment.

When Bjorn at last regained his color and the physician was satisfied that no heart anomaly caused the fall, we were released. Lunch was way overdue, so we enjoyed one more meal with the boys after all. Two points for the parents.

Following such an accident, our bond of love feels stronger, and our gratitude for one another comes out in joking and poking fun. Bjorn's blond hair was stuck up in spikes streaked with dried blood, anime-style, so we teased him about looking like pictures he used to draw. Karl-Jon accepted a ribbing for being in such a hurry to get rid of his parents, only to have us back for the entire day. Plus, he admitted hearing a *thunk* in the middle of the night but turning over and going back to sleep. We razzed him for not looking out for his brother. After lunch, back at the dorm, we rearranged Bjorn's furniture, this time with a much lower bed that had a side rail.

And eventually we were off. The boys settled into college life, and no one fell out of bed again that I know of. On the long drive home, I kept searching for God's peace, realizing that far worse things can happen to our children. This unnerving fact still haunts me anytime I let scary thoughts in.

The question is, how do I respond faithfully in the face of potential harm to my beloved children? Do I live in fear? Do I gripe at God when bad things happen? Do I implore the children over and over to be careful? Yes, they would probably tell you that I do. But I also read and reread John 27:14: "Peace I leave with you; my peace I give you. I do not give to you as the world gives. Do not let your hearts be troubled and do not be afraid." *Hmm…*

In wavering moments, when I let fear invade my mind, those words from John may dance unhelpfully on the page. That's when I must choose. Do I welcome doubts, embracing dark fears that are all too eager to fill my soul? Or will I take the words of Jesus, offered in love to His disciples when they were gripped with terror, and let them have sway over my worried mind?

Logically, the latter is my best bet, my only hope for surviving this season of sending children off to their own lives, where potential dangers exist. I will not stop praying for their protection, and I will not stop praying for my faith to hold strong, anchored in the kind of peace only God can supply.

15

Panini Parents

Surely God is my help,
the Lord is the one who sustains me.

PSALM 54:4

This simple verse from the Psalms, and ones similar to it, tell us to hang in there when the responsibilities of life feel particularly taxing. During this season when young adult children are flying from home, it's not uncommon to feel caught between concerns for them and the growing needs of our aging parents.

Recently, I was back in my hometown, helping clean out my parents' home of forty-seven years. My dad, at eighty-nine, finally decided the house is too much, and he needs to be near his daughters. Naturally, unearthing layers of memories and emotions while culling through five generations of keepsakes is hard work. While my siblings and I know this is the best decision for our dad, we feel terrible pulling him away from all that is familiar. Old friendships forged over many years, his church, and wonderful newer neighbors are precious to him. He is the oldest person on his wooded block near an elementary school, where he walks in all weather, for exercise and to talk with anyone who is out.

As homemade cooking has the power to do, Dad's oatmeal cookies forge friendships with many children and their open-hearted parents, who look out for Dad in our absence and in the absence of my late mother. Part of me feels terribly mean for uprooting him. This aching tug in my heart as we negotiate a move is the pain of parent-care.

One evening, after a full day of sorting and packing, our overwhelming job was happily broken up by our dear friend Joy and her mom, Aunt Jean, who brought us supper. What a gift! This dinner basket, obviously made out of great love on a hot day, contained many delicious dishes. Grilled pineapple pork chops, couscous, veggie skewers, fruit salad, and even homemade buttery lemon bars. (Okay, food really speaks to me!) But more important, beyond the fabulous meal, was Joy's compassionate heart. She happened to be in town to help her recently widowed mom with some new and confusing health problems, and she understood the challenges we felt.

Out of earshot of our parents, we conferred in a few furtive words, "Joy, we really *are* the sandwich generation, trying to care for our parents *and* children!"

Joy stifled a laugh, and in a muffled but heartfelt whisper added, "Sandwich? I feel like a *panini*! We're squished between trying to help our kids at the same time that the pressure of our parents' increasing needs are pressing down hard!"

I get it! Yes, a panini, where heat and pressure warms ham, melts cheese and tomatoes, and browns the bread. Joy and I and many others are in the panini press for sure, trying to be effective encouragers and problem solvers for offspring and parents alike.

It's scorching hot in the panini press, where butter on the bread sizzles. And it's *hot* in middle age, where the needs of the generations on both sides don't let up.

Joy and I didn't formulate any ingenious solutions to our predicament, but putting some of these desperate feelings into words, and better yet, laughing over them with a faithful friend, was therapeutic. Just saying, "This is not easy, but God will give us strength," lifted my spirits. On that day, barbecued pork chops from a friend helped me realize I am not in the panini press alone.

Later that night, I mentioned to my husband that we have a lot on our plate—our work, church, his parents (who also live near us), my dad, our children, our home, relationships with neighbors and other friends, and each other. I said to him, "How do we pay attention to everything and everyone?"

My ever-steady husband answered, "We don't. We take care of that which is most important, and we table the rest for later. For when the demands are a little less."

Despite my tendency to want to solve everything immediately, I suppose he is right. As sure as summer follows spring, this season of life will change. In the meantime, we must hang on to God's promise that He will be our greatest help and sustain us. Perseverance, endurance, faith, and love are what we need in this panini season.

And as we care for children and for moms and dads who require our assistance more and more, I believe it's wise to let the next generation see what we are up to. They need to have a peek into the steaming panini press to see what challenges we face. These are not their problems to solve—my siblings and I take responsibility for helping Dad move—but our children need not be shielded from the daunting demands we handle. And if they are able to lend a hand, all the better for everyone.

When it's our kids' turn to be pressed between their children and us, it will serve them well to know what they might be up against. It's one more way we help them grow up. And while we can't teach them exactly how stretched one might feel between helping parents and helping children, at least they won't be completely broadsided by the heat of the panini press when it is their turn.

Until then, let's continue to remember that God is the one who sustains us in the crazy moments when we aren't sure who needs our assistance more—the kids who are beginning their adult lives, or our parents who are nearing the finish line. May we cheer at both ends of the race. While we are somewhere in the middle, may we unswervingly run with assurance that God is our help.

16

The Empty-Nest Watershed

That person is like a tree planted by streams of water,
which yields its fruit in season
and whose leaf does not wither—
whatever they do prospers.

PSALM 1:3

I woke up today thinking about water—beautiful bodies of water, and the water that flows freely from our faucets that makes our coffee and cleans us up. Perhaps it was the route my husband and I drove yesterday from southern Nebraska north to Minnesota, crossing streams and rivers and eventually bringing us home to the land of deep blue lakes.

I thought back to last summer, when we traversed small mountains with granite slopes in northern Vermont. As we hiked up, water trickled gently down on the rock under our feet but also cascaded loudly in powerful waterfalls alongside our path. In some places, the water dropped thirty feet, and sun danced off the spray, creating little rainbows between the forest's foliage and its mossy floor. We became more aware than ever of the watershed in which we walked, awed by its beauty that was simultaneously bombastic and gentle, enormous and minute.

Geographically, we all exist in a watershed, all the time. The word simply refers to the way water in an area collects and is carried by gravity from high elevations to low. Rain falls and snow melts, forming puddles that flow into small creeks that eventually join larger streams and rivers and perchance a lake. Eventually they find their way to the ocean. The topography of the land forms the boundaries of watersheds and ultimately decides the trajectory of each water molecule. It is the ridge that regulates flow.

Because a watershed directs the course of streaming water, the word "watershed" is also used figuratively to describe a turning point. Having a baby is a watershed experience, and so is facing the empty nest. It is a time of change—a time of adjusting to a new situation. One day we wake up startled by a quiet house and a looser schedule.

Like water on the mountain that is divided and directed to spill into one basin or another, we must choose which side of the ridge we will take. It's time for intentional decision making about our life. Water seems to flow haphazardly, but its journey is guided by gravity and anything in its way, be it rock, ridge, roots, or buildings. What do we encounter along the way of our journey through the watershed?

Does a heavy heart of loss throw boulders on our path? If

so, will I deeply mourn the loss of having children at home and eventually move on to a fresh season of asking God what He would like my next focus to be?

With children out of the nest, choices of how to spend our time may be greater than they have been for years. This is freeing. But it may also feel overwhelming, like staring at a menu that is so vast it's difficult to choose what to order for dinner. And we might feel pressured to hurry up and order; after all, everyone else has already chosen what they want.

But I think we are wise to slow down, to sit with Jesus and talk with Him about this crazy watershed of the empty nest that begs a decision about what is next. It is a good time to tell Him about the longing in our hearts. Perhaps a particular cause has piqued our interest, but because our main focus has been raising children, it has remained on the back burner. Or maybe it is hidden in a remote corner of the basement.

When I first sloshed in the watershed of my empty nest, it was painfully compounded by relocation and all the loss that comes with moving. In our new town and temporary housing, I agonized for months about what to do next. I asked God over and over, "Where will we live? Who will be my new friends? Where will I work? What am I supposed to do?"

I remember one bitter cold December night, trudging through the dark around our neighborhood of identical townhouses, tears streaming down my face. I begged God for direction. I felt very alone in the land of "Minnesota nice," which I angrily told God was not nice enough or warm enough for this girl who had grown accustomed to mid-Southern living. I told Him he may have called my husband to a great new job, but now I was jobless, and I had lost my people and my purpose. The kids had moved on, and I felt abandoned. I wanted to phone a close friend back in Kansas City, but I would have only cried. I was too distraught to talk to anyone but God.

In the following months, I tromped that walk many times, sometimes in the bright sunshine of morning, and still a few more times after dark to conceal my tears. I poured out my grief, I prayed my questions, and I plodded along, winding down the watershed to new places God was giving me.

I have to remember still—I am that person who is the tree, planted by streams of water…and I will bear fruit in the right season, perhaps better for all my tears and sadness…and my leaf will not dry up and wither. And with God's help, I will prosper.

We must decide how this watershed of the empty-nest season will spur us on. Even if we stay in the location where we have always been, remaining in the same job we've had for years, it is a time to take stock of where we are and to consider what God may be calling us to do.

When children leave, a certain vacuum remains and begs to be filled. If we don't fill it intentionally and thoughtfully with good things, it will fill willy-nilly with whatever comes along. I've watched some empty-nest moms default to mindless hours in front of the TV, sipping chardonnay by the bottleful. Or searching for fulfillment at the mall, the salon, or many insipid ladies' nights out. There's nothing wrong with shopping or getting a haircut or going to happy hour with the gals, but these might not be the most fulfilling endeavors after all.

As God became very near to me in the murky moments of my emptiness, He also answered my desperate cries for community and worthwhile work. It didn't happen overnight, and some of it I still struggle to understand. But as sure as water flows from top to bottom, God walked with me, sliding with me through the watershed from one place and season to the next.

I am grateful for new friendships and new work. They are not like what I had in Washington, DC, or Kansas City, where we raised our children, but they are answers to prayer. Strong friendships of the heart don't develop overnight. Patience is required. But by never letting go of Jesus's hand, the journey is possible and sometimes even pleasant. On the darkest nights, I never thought I would say so.

One more reference to water comes from the words of Jesus Himself. He tells a Samaritan woman at Jacob's well, "Everyone who drinks this water will be thirsty again, but whoever drinks the water I give him will never thirst. Indeed, the water I give will become a spring of water welling up to eternal life" (John 4:13-14).

As empty-nest mothers, may we say yes to Jesus and gratefully drink the living water that He so generously offers.

17

Faith Walk...
Not a Cakewalk

*Faith is being sure of what we hope for
and certain of what we do not see.*

HEBREWS 11:1

Releasing children into the world is a painful struggle for even the strongest and most stoic mother. Eighteen-year-olds feel so wise, invincible, and bold, ready to take the world by storm as they zoom out of the house in fearless conquering mode. It's a funny thing how eighteen or twenty feels like a wise, ripe age when that *is* your age. But double that number, and in hindsight eighteen or twenty seems very young. No doubt you've done your best to pour knowledge and experience into your kids' lives, but now that launch day has arrived, you secretly fear, "Did I do enough? Will they survive living away from home?" And what do you do with the college kid who offhandedly mentions they plan to study in Japan, France, Sweden, or Turkey? Or what about that child who announces that the Army is sending them to Afghanistan or that the Peace Corps assigned them to Mali?

If you're like me, you smile and nod the nod of confidence at this son or daughter. You reassuringly communicate your feelings of pride and confidence in their ability to succeed so far from home. Inside, however, your heart is quaking, and your stomach is doing flip-flops of the most nauseating kind. "Ja-p-p-pan," I heard my voice quiver as my son told me he was already registered at a school northeast of Osaka.

Panicky thoughts at moments such as these stretch our faith in our kids and also in God. How do we know they will be safe? How do we know they will find their way around in a country whose language they barely speak? Well…we don't! That is what *faith* is all about. Hebrews 11:1 says, "Faith is confidence in what we hope for and assurance about what we do not see." It is a step of faith to put that son or daughter on an international flight by himself or herself.

The nervous pre-boarding moments at the airport are when I manage to unwittingly irritate my kids the most. I ask them for the third time if they have their passport and foreign currency. I remind them to keep their wallet in a safe place as they inch through security, and their eyes roll toward the ceiling. Relinquishing all control is such a struggle. The protective mother-bond, woven thick and strong, must now loosen for our fledglings to take flight.

So if our kids are enticed by wanderlust, let's be strong enough to give them the freedom to fly. At the same time, may we grab hold of faith—both in our children, whom we have trained, and in Jesus, who cares for them wherever they roam and in whatever terrifying situations they find themselves. This challenge of believing in what we cannot see is at the core of what God wants *us* to know. He calls us to release our children into His care, where they will make decisions and solve problems on their own. But they are not the only ones who will learn big lessons. As moms, we take a gigantic step into deeper faith with our heavenly Father.

18

Care Packages

Casting all your care upon him;
for he careth for you.

1 Peter 5:7 kjv

As a little girl, I had a plaque on the wall in my bedroom. It had a picture of a frog on it because I was a weird kid who liked frogs. It said, "He careth for you (1 Peter 5:7)." I wonder how many times I read those words as I ran in and out of my room. I imagine I subconsciously took it in. However it happened, I grew up knowing that God loved and cared for me very much.

When I consider all the ways God shows His deep love and care for each of us, I am amazed. Again, thinking back to childhood, I remember an unusual, vivid encounter with Christ on a very ordinary night. I was about seven, and it was sometime during the Christmas season. It wasn't Christmas Eve or December seventh, my birthday, which were typically nights when my heart was thumping too fast to fall asleep. It had nothing to do with presents or parties, having Christmas company, or baking cookies. I just remember waking up in the night and being very alert. I was aware of my sister in the bed next to me and of the dark and quiet in the house. I wasn't used to waking up in the middle of the night, and I tried to go back to sleep. But I couldn't.

Rather than review my Christmas list and the probability of receiving a desired gift—my normal childish progression of thoughts in December—my mind went to the story of Jesus's birth. With pictures out of a storybook leading me on, I mentally took the entire journey with Mary and Joseph. I could see them going to Bethlehem, only to be disappointed by inns that had no available rooms. I had a lot of pity for them since motels with No Vacancy signs were a common occurrence for my family on vacation. But for the expectant couple to find a barn, where Mary could have the baby in a bed of straw, seemed much better. I'm sure I romanticized the situation because I loved barns and the animals in them. After all, *Charlotte's Web* constructed my view of agrarian life in second grade, and I saw it as warm and delightful.

I thought about baby Jesus's birth and about the angels telling the shepherds to visit the Christ child, and I saw golden light that glowed from inside the stable. Mary was serene and beautiful, and Joseph, strong and protective, looked a lot like my own father, except with a beard. In my mind's eye, the wise men came earlier than they did in real life, bringing their gifts, shiny and valuable, causing Mary and Joseph's eyes to widen in wonder.

And the joy of the story washed over me so powerfully, I remember warm tears running into my ears and down my neck, making my pillow damp. And I felt deeply happy! It was as if the angels had come to my bedside with their great tidings of joy, and I was the only one who knew the wonder of the story. God came to me in this strange nocturnal visit to let me know that indeed, *He careth for me*. It was as if He sent a fantastic care package to me, one I was allowed to open all by myself under the covers.

For many years I have wondered about this experience that filled me with warmth and happiness. I didn't write in a journal as a second grader, but if I had, I surely would have expressed my unexpected feelings of joy and the sense of security that God's love gave. Instead, like Mary, I pondered in my heart what had happened. I'm sure I told no one about it. Until now.

Jesus, coming to earth as an innocent baby, was the greatest example of the most creative and best care package ever sent. Our heavenly Father cared about humankind so much, He sent His Son as an infant to be the Savior of the world. He knew what we needed most, and He made it happen.

I'm not for a moment suggesting that we are heavenly parents, but as empty-nest mothers, we too long to send good things to our children who may be a long way from home. Sometimes we struggle to know how best to care for our children from a distance. It's not as easy as it was when they were under our roof. But one thing most of our faraway children have is a mailbox. And who isn't overjoyed to receive a note or a care package?

I love to send care packages to our children. Not that I do it all that often; in fact, one son who is still in school could benefit from one in the next week or two.

I suppose my kids know what to expect in a box from Mom—something home-baked, mini pecan pies, homemade granola, and some useful little items, like a new toothbrush or a pair of socks. This is my chance to send a note of encouragement and maybe a gift card to their favorite coffee shop. A bag of freshly roasted coffee beans makes the box smell really great, and if there's room, I'll tuck in a jar of jam from the summer. Chocolate is a must, as are dried fruits, and nuts, and some xylitol gum to save their teeth from the goodies. We all know what our kids like or what they may want to share with a roommate. Perhaps nut butters, grainy crackers, Nutella, or tea.

The worst part is the cost of postage nowadays. But I figure how much less our grocery bills are with kids out of the house and justify the expense that way. Plus, I use flat-rate postage boxes and fill them to the max. Simple little treats from home, packed by Mom, go a long way to convey love.

Sometimes I have wondered if I enjoy filling care packages more than our kids like getting them. But last spring I received a phone call that put an end to that misled thought.

Karl-Jon, who is pushing hard through a demanding graduate program, called home breathless and excited. That afternoon, as he sat exhausted, listening to another student give a final presentation, his professor, who sat next to him, leaned over and said, "Hey, Karl-Jon, congratulations!"

In shock, he whispered, "For what?"

"Don't you read your email?"

After pulling another all-nighter, he honestly replied, "Not this morning."

"You were awarded the research fellowship."

This was a huge honor, pushing him in his exhausted state to tears. He jumped up, ran out of class for a moment, and called me with the amazing news. It was an effort to grasp the goodness of this unexpected blessing. He thanked me for my encouragement throughout the year. But what surprised me most were his words, "I wouldn't have made it through without the care packages you sent." Oh, my goodness! I cried as well.

We can send love to our kids in many ways. In spoken words, in a handwritten note, in a text, or in a care package. But I hadn't realized how much weight they carry. Suddenly, I feel more motivated than ever to bake, pack, and mail a box to that same grad student, who is in the thick of it once again.

And as I do, I think of that extraordinary care package from God—the reality of Jesus's birth—that He sent to me when I was a child needing reassurance of His love. And like my son, I too am grateful and wouldn't make it through without such a gift.

19

The Original Empty Nest

These three remain, faith, hope and
love. But the greatest of these is love.

1 CORINTHIANS 13:13

In the beginning of our marriage, my husband and I settled happily into our first home together on Chicago's north side. We were fresh back from our honeymoon, a week in the hills of Kentucky followed by a few days on the shore of Lake Michigan. By heading south in mid-October, we held on to summer's warmth and sunshine, and as we drove north to the lake, the world was aglow with red and yellow maples and spikes of evergreens tucked in between.

It was a glorious time; everything was new and exciting. Our cozy apartment, the upstairs of an old house, was perfect for us. It was 550 square feet of hardwood floors, sloping dormers, plenty of sunshine, and character. We opened our wedding gifts and gave each a place in one of the four rooms. What fun it was to hang pictures, stack dishes in the pantry, and put our clothes away in the same closet. My new husband was quick to install dimmer switches and build a few pieces of furniture. We joked that we felt like two kids playing house, which in retrospect, wasn't far from the truth. We were building our nest, and it was incredibly fun!

We were fortunate that our honeymoon apartment remained our home for four years. Many of our newlywed friends were on the move, but we needed to stay put to finish our degrees, which was just fine with us. Not only did we have the opportunity to grow academically, we had time to meld together as a couple. We married young, and in a sense, we grew up together. During these married-student years, we weathered disappointments and real-life tragedy. Lack of money caused me to pass on the graduate program I really wanted. My brother died, and my grandfather followed not long after. Our studies were demanding, and we wedged as many hours of work into each week as we could. We shed some tears over our finances and ate a lot of beans, but we always paid our rent on time. We learned about the expectations we had for ourselves and for each other, and we discovered we each had our distinct ways to solve problems. Sometimes we misunderstood one other, but we were in love and incredibly grateful to be together.

This was our original empty nest. It was the two of us, finding our way, figuring things out as a couple rather than as individuals. Sure, we were still two separate people, studying different subjects, honing specific skills. But we did it side by side, paying attention to what the other was doing. Eric quizzed me in anatomy and physiology, and I read some of his papers on theology and the New Testament. We joined a church and a small group and learned to mingle our prayers.

Most evenings, we cooked, ate at our kitchen table, did the dishes, and returned to the college library to study until it closed. But once in a while we tossed the books aside and went to bed early, so grateful to be husband and wife.

Those years of playing house and enjoying the newness of marriage were the bedrock from which we moved into careers and parenting. Naturally, life became more complicated with jobs and three babies. Our list of responsibilities grew, and we weren't just "playing house" anymore.

Sometimes late at night following a hectic day, after the children were in bed, I made a pot of chocolate fondue and surrounded it with berries. I brought it up to our bedroom on a silver platter that was a wedding gift, and we sat in bed, dipping berries in chocolate, remembering our empty nest when it was just the two of us and our days were a little more carefree.

As the children's school years approached, life switched into fast-forward. Toddlers were suddenly in preschool and then kindergarten. And that was just the beginning of frenetic, fun-filled years of raising kids. Some days seemed achingly long, but the years zipped by like the cars of a speeding train. As Mom and Dad, we tried to do what was best for our children and for each other. Sometimes we got it right, and sometimes we didn't.

Even today, with our children out of the nest, we must decide what risks are worth taking. It is a balancing act as we attempt to keep many balls in the air at once. The pieces we juggle include children, church (which is Eric's work as well as our spiritual home and the center of many friendships), my work, extended family, the kids' educations, and relationships with others in our community. And of course, there is our home and our marriage.

In this list, marriage is at the end, but certainly not because it is least important. However, I regret to say that sometimes I let many things come ahead of it. But thank goodness my husband does not. He has kept our relationship afloat through thick and thin by making it a priority. I am enormously grateful because that is really where my heart is as well.

When I was a young mom and taught childbirth classes to expectant parents, I always ended the six-week series with one strong message. I told each group of parents that after all the tools they learned to help with the birth and to care for their newborn, the best thing they can do for their baby is to guard the love they have for each other. Keep a date night. Grab snatches of time together—chocolate fondue—whenever you can. Light candles. Kindle the romance. Remember what pleases your spouse.

Two parents faced away from each other for at least two decades, giving attention only to children and professions, is a common tragedy. These well-intentioned, hardworking couples may hold only splinters of a marriage by the time they see the last kiddo out of the nest. But even if that is the case, if two are still together, there is hope.

By the time the second empty nest comes around, we have weathered many storms. We have taken risks. Some turned out to be good ones…others, not so much. Or we have not taken certain risks, which we regret. We all get beat up in one way or another—with disappointments, or with just plain exhaustion. We are not the same youngsters who played house years ago. But we need to remember that something wonderful drew us together in the beginning, and that something is vitally important.

When was the last time you pulled out your wedding photos to look at them together? I know, it takes time. And if your marriage has been on the rocks, or if the person you are married to has become just a nice roommate, it might feel too risky. But if that is the case, what have you got to lose? I'm all for trading what is mediocre for something new, beautiful, and grand.

Even this weekend, with a load of work and responsibilities piled on our heads, my husband and I struggle to find time to celebrate our anniversary. We have had so much to do lately, visiting infirmed parents, doing our jobs, and caring for others. Our house needs winterizing. We see that the list of chores isn't going to let up anytime soon. But we are going to celebrate by having supper out, just the two of us. We will take time to remember what a good idea it was to get married way back when.

We will celebrate the goodness of our second empty nest and a return to freedom. We love it when our children come home and we are reunited as a family, but we also enjoy being just us. We are the slightly older version of newlyweds who whistled to each other from the sidewalk below our first apartment. We will remind each other to keep the faith and hope in our future together. And best of all, we will celebrate our love, which is the greatest gift we give each other.

20

The Best Kind of Rest

*Come to me all who are weary and burdened, and
I will give you rest. Take my yoke upon you and
learn from me, for I am gentle and humble in
heart, and you will find rest for your souls. For
my yoke is easy and my burden is light.*

MATTHEW 11:28-30

As empty-nest mothers, finding rest for our weary souls is not necessarily easy. Even this morning, I awoke extra early and couldn't go back to sleep. This happens frequently as my mind wanders to children who are far away, whose challenges I know only bits about. I also think of our parents, who live close by and need more care than we are sometimes able to give.

Saint Augustine wrote in his fourth-century autobiography, "Thou hast made us for Thyself and our hearts are restless till they rest in Thee."[1]

My heart is restless, all right. I rearrange the duck down in my pillow and try to pinpoint what is keeping me awake. What troubles my mind this time? Children? Parents? Deadlines? I lie still in the predawn darkness, hours before the birds begin to sing. The tiny light on the smoke detector blinks above our bedroom door. Suddenly I remember that our boys each live in second-story apartments in ancient wooden houses that are the best each can afford near the schools they attend. Do they have functional smoke detectors? My heart rate increases, and I make a mental note to inquire about this the next time we talk. Immediately my thoughts fly to care packages that are well overdue, and I wonder if I can fit cookie baking into the day's busy schedule. And while my little mind races on and sleep eludes, I realize I am dog tired.

I think back to Augustine. "Our hearts don't rest until they *rest* in Thee."

Another insightful author, David Benner, responds to Jesus's invitation to take His yoke upon us and to learn from Him. He says that as he draws near to Jesus, his heart is more aligned with the heart of God, which in turn allows God's desires to become his desires and God's will to become his own.[2] In other words, this much-needed *rest* is the result of being aware of God's presence and taking a step toward Him. He is always present, but sometimes our awareness is lacking.

All too often I hold tight to my worries and don't let anyone in—not even Jesus. I walk under the weight of a heavy pack that contains large rocks of concern. And I am stubborn and determined to do this by myself. I reason, "I got myself into this or that mess, and I alone must get myself out," but that attitude is my undoing. I miss the fact that Jesus walks alongside, willingly takes the pack from my back, and places it on His own. He does this even in the midst of the fevered pace at which I move. But I need to stop so He can wiggle the pack from my shoulders, open it up, and dig around to see what I have shoved inside. He understands the concerns I have made so important and weighty. He knows what robs me of rest.

"Take my yoke upon you." Have you ever wondered about this yoke? Picture a curvy horizontal piece of wood with two loops hanging down. They fit around the necks of a pair of oxen. We are more likely to have seen one on the wall of a barbecue restaurant than attached to oxen in a field. The yoke keeps the oxen together as they pull heavy cargo in unison, sharing the weight of their burden. Thus the work is lighter for each ox. Similarly, you and I can be connected to Jesus, realizing that in His amazing love, He helps shoulder the loads we carry.

He is with us in loneliness, heartbreak, overly demanding schedules, and worry that keeps us awake. Our souls need rest in Jesus even if we are called to swift action that feels like anything but rest.

Last Sunday, my husband and I planned some rest time after a highly scheduled weekend. It was our thirty-fifth anniversary, and we had dinner reservations at a lovely French restaurant. We planned to first bring supper to my father because he recently fell and cannot get out. On the way, however, we received a call saying that my dear father-in-law, who suffers with Alzheimer's, fell down at his care center and split open a place on the back of his head. It needed stitches, and they asked us if we could come and take him to the emergency room.

"Yes, of course," I told his nurse. "We are on our way."

After dropping dinner at my dad's, we proceeded to find my father-in-law, Paul, who was sitting propped up in a wheelchair like a Civil War casualty with gauze encircling his head. He looked so small, just a shadow of the strong man he used to be.

We pushed back our dinner reservation.

It was a struggle to get Paul into the car. He had not ridden anywhere since the last time he went down hard and needed sutures. And instead of a French restaurant, we found ourselves at the hospital, waiting for a doctor to come in and examine Paul's wound, which now seeped blood through the gauze. We changed our dinner reservation again when it became evident that this would take some time.

At last, a knock at the door signaled help had arrived. We expected the doctor or nurse to come in to assess the injury. Instead, we were amazed to discover dear friends who came to toast our anniversary right there in the tiny emergency examining room. They witnessed Paul's fall while visiting their mother in the same nursing home and realized what was going on.

What fun to see them! They brought cheese and crackers and a bubbly beverage, which we enjoyed together while Dad dozed, oblivious to the mini-party alongside his bed.

The next one to be surprised was the doctor who came to care for Paul. He didn't expect an anniversary celebration either. He was wonderful as he gently and skillfully cleaned and closed the wound with staples. Paul took it all very well. Eventually we loaded him back into the car and drove him to his care facility, where his kind nurse settled him in for the night.

Our dinner was in serious jeopardy by this time, but we pushed our reservation as late as we dared and headed downtown, still hopeful.

The restaurant was very accommodating. When at last we collapsed in exhaustion at our candlelit table for two to celebrate our anniversary, we looked at each other and exhaled deeply. "How did the demands of life mushroom to such a level?"

What a rollercoaster of emotion surrounds such an evening. It is heartbreaking to care for a loved one who no longer knows who we are. It is painful to see him in pain. We feel helpless as the two of us can barely lift Dad into our car. We can't make him understand what is going on, but we recognize his endearing mannerisms and beautiful blue eyes. The rest of the clouded Alzheimer's mind is as foreign to us as we are to him. We feel like crying.

But then we are cheered by friends who are walking a similar walk with their dear mother. In their surprise visit, our spirits are buoyed by their kindness. We laugh and smile in the midst of the sadness. We feel loved; we are less weary.

At the restaurant, we take in the splendor around us and the beauty of being just the two of us, celebrating three and a half decades of steady married love. We order dinner and giggle that by God's grace this meal is happening at all.

Resting in Jesus…even in moments of crisis, disappointment, and messed-up plans. It is in Him that we will survive the crazy demands of caring for our parents, whose list of needs could fill a legal pad.

Resting in Jesus…breathing a prayer when the phone rings with the next big or little crisis that requires our immediate attention. Staying calm, not freaking out when we go to Plan C or D.

Resting in Jesus…hungering for Him. It is a choice! And once the habit is solid, it becomes an absolute necessity. Let us attach ourselves to the yoke that offers a place for two. One for Jesus and one for us. This journey is not to be taken alone. It is hard. It requires our whole heart with all of our energy plugged into Him.

I daresay we appreciated our dinner date more because it almost didn't happen. But what we will probably remember most are our friends who popped into the emergency room, ready to make our evening special no matter what. Their loving presence proved they understand what we are going through. We are comforted to know they share our journey. They showed up as friends in the flesh, but they brought the spirit of Christ and helped us rest in Him, even as we held our father's hand and tried to ease his pain.

21

Bring Them Safely Home

Do not be anxious about anything, but in everything
by prayer and petition, with thanksgiving, present
your requests to God. And the peace of God,
which transcends all understanding, will guard
your hearts and your minds in Christ Jesus.

Philippians 4:6-7

Whether the journey takes them across town, to the other side of the country, or to a far-flung continent, our off-spring are on the move. Maybe you have one who flies to a coast for basic training, or to a new job or internship, or off to college, with no plans to come home until Thanksgiving or Christmas. A pattern of children circling in and out develops for each family while parents' emotions wax and wane with each homecoming and inevitable farewell. Airports and train stations crawl with young adults over the holidays. For every backpack that bobs up and down along concourse and platform, I imagine a mother waiting for the first glimpse of her son or daughter to come home. And I envision clouds of prayers that hover around, mothers begging God for safe journeys.

Today I am one of those mothers as I pray travel mercies over our children. We have a wonderful weekend upon us, in which our three will arrive home to celebrate a friend's wedding. Johanna will drive six hours from upper Michigan in her tired old Subaru; Bjorn and Karl-Jon will fly home from Boston and Charlottesville, Virginia, rendezvousing at the airport after midnight. My heart bubbles with joy to think of our twentysomethings gathered around our kitchen table for a long, leisurely breakfast tomorrow morning. This is a rare, rare treat, to be just the five of us for a couple of days. Most homecomings include a lot of extended family together at a beach house or jammed into our house for Christmas. These gatherings that include cousins, aunts and uncles, and grandparents are filled with exuberant glee, but to be the original mom, dad, and three children is a special treat, and I am bursting with anticipation!

But as they travel by car and by plane, low-level butterflies flutter in my stomach, and I mumble at Jesus all day long. I have gotten very specific in my prayers for safe journeys. I ask God that no harm will come to our traipsing loved ones. I pray they don't lose anything along the way, and I especially plead with God that I will hear their footsteps on the front porch, announcing they are safe and sound.

I am not superstitious as I choose the words of my prayers. I have no power to prevent calamity of any sort, but in being faithful to prayer itself, I tell God that we desire our children have no serious trouble as they travel. I admit that a shadow hovers over my prayers for journey mercies, so I lift up particular words for God to watch over our three on the road and in the air.

Why such specific requests, one might ask? It's fair to say that life experiences influence our approach to many things, and that is the case for me when it comes to travel. Today, the explicit nature of my prayers is born out of praying for my little brother to arrive home from his college spring break when I was in my midtwenties. My husband and I were still students in Chicago, and it was our spring break as well. Our whole family was tremendously excited to welcome my brother and sister home—Jon from school in Texas, and Kris from her job in California. Jon flew to meet Kris, and they began their long trek across the great West to Chicago.

The day before their anticipated arrival, my husband and I got up early, put together unusually elaborate plates of food, and jumped back under our down comforter to enjoy breakfast in bed. We prayed a quick prayer for Jon and Kris to have a safe cross-country drive and smiled at the vacation morning with no class or clinicals.

At about halfway through breakfast, my mother called. I picked it up and heard her sobbing, and I knew something was terribly wrong. Mom *never* sounded like this before. Then she delivered the deathblow: "It's Jon…"

"O God! What?" My mind struggled to make sense of her words. I crumpled to the floor, finding it difficult to breathe. In the next few seconds I imagined a car wreck; a semi crossing the center line, landing my sister in critical condition.

"Mom, what about Krissy?"

"She is fine. He fell."

"O Lord, have mercy! *NO!*" I remembered they were camping at the Grand Canyon on the way.

"Mom," I sobbed, "are you alone?"

"No. Pastor Wiens is here. But you must go to your dad's office and tell him."

Mechanically I told her we would, but I had no idea how to do such a dreadful thing. Eric held me and then helped me into the shower, where I screamed at God. The smell of the shampoo I used that morning makes me nauseous to this day.

Eric drove; I held my knees to my chest and concentrated on breathing in and breathing out. We might just as well have shot my dad with a gun than tell him his young son was dead. I shudder to remember how the news threw him from his chair. He hit his head on a file cabinet. It was all Eric and I could do to pick him up from his office floor, help him to our car, and drive him home to my waiting mother.

The valley of the shadow of death swallowed each of us. My family of origin is not large; we have no first cousins. But our church family surrounded us with incredible love. One by one, friends filed in through the back door, the unofficial, official doorway for friends. They sat with us. They fed us. They loved us and kept faith when ours failed. And we waited.

We waited for my sister to fly home from Flagstaff. And we waited for my brother's remains to arrive at O'Hare. Fortunately, they came on separate flights. My older brother and his wife joined us, broken and stunned, and we waited for my sister to arrive.

When at last we were together and Krissy could tell us exactly what happened at the canyon, our hearts broke in unison. And then my father did the most beautiful thing. He pulled us together in a huddle and lifted his busted voice in prayer, asking God to receive Jon into His loving arms.

Over the next few days, hundreds of friends came to celebrate the vibrant, faithful life of Jonathan Bladel, a true follower and servant of Christ. He lived more life in twenty-one years than some people do in eighty. We praised God; we thanked Him for an extraordinary brother, son, grandson, and friend. We comforted each other the best we could. When words felt inadequate, loving looks and squeezed hands took over. The body of Christ breathed life when all we could see was life ended.

But that was the easy part. What is much more difficult is the way life rushes on when everyone leaves. Commerce throbs, deadlines loom. Demanding classes resumed for Eric and me, and for my older brother, Randy, and his wife, Julie. Randy had to take med-school boards two weeks later. I was furious.

We had prayed for safety! My parents had prayed, and my husband and I prayed together, out loud, for Krissy and Jon to come safely home. I was devastated. Praying seemed futile. After all, what good are prayers that end in calamity?

The shattered pieces of our lives after Jon's death have taken years to come back together for our family. As in all griefs, our healing comes unevenly. Healing itself is snagged with pain and doubt. But part of the mending came to myself and my family in the last words Jon wrote in his journal the night before he died. At the canyon, tucked into his sleeping bag in a two-person tent with my sister, he wrote by flashlight, "….and please aid safety." At first his words, scrawled in his familiar endearing penmanship, were salt on weeping wounds.

I wanted to shout, "You didn't do it, God! You failed us. He asked for safety and fell to his death less than twenty-four hours later. Didn't You care? Don't You care now?"

But then I thought about my free-spirited little brother, who enjoyed thrilling adventure, which caused the rest of us to pray extra for him. He was the one who took off for the wilds of Alaska to help missionaries build a hangar and earn a pilot's license at nineteen.

It took years, but eventually I noticed that though I missed Jon terribly, I didn't worry about him anymore. I didn't need to. He was safe. He is the only one of us who really *is* safe. God did bring him safely home; it just wasn't the home we had in mind. Instead of coming home to us, he arrived at his ultimate home with Jesus.

But now that I am the mother praying for my children to reach home tonight without incident, I remind God to be gentle and merciful with our children, and if it is His will, I ask God to deliver them to us without harm.

Going back to the same God who I felt profoundly let me down when I was twenty-five may not make sense, but it is the only thing I can do.

For as crushed and flattened as I felt by Jon's death, I was saved by a moment of joyful light that split the cavern of darkness when my dad embraced us and asked God to take Jon's spirit to Himself. In the midst of fresh grief, in a nanosecond of even fresher hope, I remember a twinge of inexplicable joy.

"Please aid safety." The words of Jon, answered by God, encouraging us to not be anxious about anything, but in everything by prayer and petition, with thanksgiving, to present our requests to God. And the peace of God, which transcends all understanding, will guard our hearts and minds in Christ Jesus (Philippians 4:6-7).

It may not seem logical, but what in this life does? In every struggle, we must choose to keep our faith or to chuck it. After losing Jon, I was angry that God let us down. But He is not a great-grandfather in heaven who jumps to answer all my prayers the way I want. He could choose to miraculously break the rules of gravity that He put in place, but in the case of my brother, He did not.

Rather, He promises to walk with us in the midst of dashed hopes in the valley of death. So I will go with faith. It is all I have to hang my hope upon, for surely someday, the joy of ultimate everlasting safety will outshine the temporary goodness of being together in the here and now.

22

The Classics, My Early Morning Friends

Be still, and know that I am God.

Psalm 46:10

The greatest benefit of living in an empty nest greets me first thing every morning. It is *silence*! As much as I used to love waking up to the cooing of a sweet baby, or to children padding around and hunting for breakfast in footie pajamas, or even to high schoolers who gobble French toast and run, the quiet of today is wonderful.

In complete darkness, I head to the kitchen, push the magic button on our coffeemaker that is set up ready to brew, and exercise while the coffee wafts its heavenly fragrance throughout the house. Only after muscles are stretched and strengthened will I pour a cup of java, take to my favorite corner of the couch, and turn on a light. Instantly, my stack of books is illuminated, and I am ready to meet my "friends."

First I encounter whatever character is in the portion of the Bible I am reading on any given day. Lately I've been poking through a version of the New Testament that is put together chronologically without chapter or verse numbers.[1] It reads more like a novel, showing me nuances in the Scriptures I never noticed before. This slight change in format opens my eyes wide to new discoveries. This alone makes getting up early worthwhile.

Next I am ready to hear from my old friends, the great classic writers of the Christian faith. The works of these believers have been carefully preserved; their sage insights stand the test of time.

Madame Jeanne Guyon (1684–1717) reminds me that God's desire to give Himself to me is greater than my desire to lay hold of Him.[2] Her words are strong and powerful, urging me to let God be my leader in all things. She boldly states, "If God is your mover, you will go much farther in a short time than all your repeated self-effort could ever do."[3] How true! And she pushes for greater depth in prayer out of her incredible experience of a prayer-centered life.

Brother Lawrence (1611–1691), who calls himself "a servant of the servants of God," endears himself to me every time I read his words. Brother Lawrence was born into low means in Lorraine, France. I imagine he knew the flavor of incredible cheese, but he never had a formal education. As he worked hard in the kitchen of the Discalced Carmelite order in Paris, Brother Lawrence practiced a constant consciousness of the presence of Christ. His exuberant inner life elevated his spirit and soul above the mundane kitchen chores that were his daily work.[4] I return to his messages over and over. He writes, "Nothing in the world is more sweet and delightful than the kind of life that is in continual conversation with God."[5] He cheers me on as I consider my own work when he says, "You must serve God in a holy freedom by doing your business faithfully without any trouble or nervousness."[6] I am grateful to Brother Lawrence for his unusual life, and to his abbot, Joseph de Beaufort, who collected Brother Lawrence's writings. They are known four centuries later as some of the most beautiful, joyful memoirs of the faith.

Another articulate writer, John of the Cross (1542–1591), draws me deeper through his *Dark Night of the Soul*.[7] If any of the classic sacred writers uncover pitfalls of the inner Christian journey, it is John of the Cross. He helps me see that the "feelings we receive from our devotional life are the least of its benefits. The invisible and unfelt grace of God is much greater, and it is beyond our comprehension."[8]

In addition to the centuries-old encouragers of the faith, more recent writers—C.S. Lewis (1900–1963) and Henri Nouwen (1932–1996)—speak to my heart. Lewis, with his no-nonsense approach to why the church exists, impresses me with his logical mind. He offers grist for thought as he says, "The Church exists for nothing else but to draw men into Christ, to make them little Christs."[9] And he proceeds, "It says in the Bible that the whole universe was made for Christ and that everything is to be gathered together in Him."[10]

And dear, humble Henri Nouwen, in his book *With Burning*

Hearts, draws me to the table, to the moment when Jesus's friends recognize Him as he breaks the bread a few days after the resurrection.[11] I savor these pages, short sections at a time, walking with the risen Savior and two friends on the road to Emmaus. Nouwen brings this story to life in a fresh way. I have known this tale for years, but never with such awareness of the fellowship Christ created as He walked and dined with friends.

Each morning one of these exemplary followers of Jesus comes to call. Their enduring words take me by the hand and lead me closer to God. Their stories provide plenty to ponder.

Mornings didn't happen in the same way when we had a houseful of children, which is why this predawn silence feels like a great bonus of the empty nest. For the many years kids reside at home, we mothers serve and solve problems from the moment our feet hit the floor. I'm not saying we don't pray and do devotions with children around, but to enjoy complete quiet for at least the first hour of each day is truly a precious gift. In solitude, I get to tell Jesus what's on my mind, and I wait quietly to hear what He wants to say to me. It's a gift to have time to pray for children and friends, parents, and those in ministry and mission. This is my chance to ask God to reveal my sins and ask forgiveness, to praise Him, and to write in my journal. And thankfully, God usually uses the morning to direct me to what He'd like me to write about that day.

I also like to watch the first birds that come to our feeder, beginning with the cardinals. As they preside over the sunflower seeds, they remind me that the Holy Spirit is always present, though invisible. Our beloved cardinals, the males in their bright red jackets and the females in a softer reddish-gray, aren't always in view either, but I know they are nearby in the trees or bracken. When they show up in all their splendor, they remind me that this is a rich time on which I have come to depend.

Ironically, this gift of early morning goodness came to me as the result of one of our children who returned home for a brief time, as I will explain.

23

The Boomers and the Boomerangs

My son, do not let wisdom and understanding out of your sight, preserve sound judgment and discretion; they will be life for you, an ornament to grace your neck. Then you will go on your way in safety, and your foot will not stumble. When you lie down, you will not be afraid; when you lie down, your sleep will be sweet.

PROVERBS 3:21-24

Today, in many homes across America, parents launch their fledglings, only to receive them back three or four years later, toting an increased number of books and, in our case, expanded collections of studio art supplies. While the parental home has historically been a refuge for young adults striving to "figure it out," in recent years this is increasingly the case. In 1975, 26 percent of young adults lived in their parents' home, but that number has climbed to about one in three today.[1] The Pew Research Center reports that according to research based on credit report data, the median estimated length of time that young adults reside once again with Mom and Dad increased from two and a half years in 2005 to three years in 2013.[2]

Economics is clearly the driving force that boomerangs students back to the nest. Most twentysomethings would rather not come home, but sometimes it is the best alternative in light of debt obligations and the cost of living independently.[3] It is also worth mentioning that less educated young adults have a higher chance of living with parents due to the low-paying jobs available to these young people.[4]

Incidentally, when I asked our daughter, Johanna, who is in her late twenties, what words of wisdom she might have for us empty-nest mothers, she immediately expressed her gratitude for parents who willingly defer the freedom of the empty nest to welcome a boomerang child back home. Johanna is speaking from experience. Since college graduation, she has returned home to work, pay off student loans, and build a little nest egg. Being frugal and diligent, she is once again back out on her own, but it was during her return that early mornings became my favorite way to start the day.

Johanna had a long commute from our home to the classroom where she taught, and in order to grab a bit of time together each day, we shared breakfast at five fifty each morning. Sometimes I was a zombie-mom, scrambling eggs in my sleep, but it was my choice. And as soon as Johanna grabbed her coffee to go, I poured mine and took to my corner of books to read and pray. This routine was my boomerang benison.

Our boys have also circled back under our roof to work

a handful of summer jobs and internships. They have saved money and broadened their employment experiences while applying to graduate schools. They are East-Coasters now, but the months when they lived with us provided special opportunities to appreciate them as the mature young men they have become. We went through more food, but that was a small price to pay for the joy of having them home for a couple of summers.

I think we all long to see our children grown up and established in their own places. But with today's economy and the astronomical cost of education, it is natural that many young adults return home for a while.

This isn't ideal in every case. When the children are home, it's natural to worry about them if they are out late or if we don't know where they are. Sometimes we get in each other's way. Each of us may head to the washing machine at the exact same moment on a Saturday morning, carrying an overflowing basket of dirty clothes. And with children who love to cook, we must talk about who is using the kitchen and who needs to clean up the cooktop. It's like having any roommate, but this time we are the homeowner trying to be gracious to children who need a temporary place to live.

My father, of the silent generation, points out that when he was twenty-five, if a child returned home, they paid rent to their parents, who often struggled to make ends meet. Each family must decide how best to handle the financial aspect of their own boomerang situation.

Of course, communication is of utmost importance. It goes

both ways. When our children are back home, I leave a note on the counter saying I'm out on a bike ride, and they do the same. We try to keep track of each other, just as any good roommate would do. Being considerate goes a long way to growing a mutually satisfying relationship with an adult child. And it helps for everyone to remember this arrangement is not forever. Mom and Dad need their space, and so do the children.

The fact that millennials are marrying later than previous generations also increases the number of young adults returning home. The average age for a first marriage has climbed steadily since 2000. Many millennials view marriage second to getting a solid education that ensures income for both partners. Some even call marriage a "strategic alliance" in which both husband and wife have good earning potential before they tie the knot. They plan to marry, but they are waiting until careers are in place.[5]

Perhaps those of us who married younger put greater emphasis on finding the right person earlier. I think it's interesting to hear what our children believe about this societal change. Here is fertile ground for conversation at the least, and an opportunity to share our thoughts as well.

Proverbs 3:21-24 encourages wisdom, understanding, sound judgment, and discretion; let's let these characteristics be present as we relate with our young adult children. And if those children boomerang back home, let's look for the blessings. Inevitably we find them if we have our eyes lovingly open to see what they are.

24

Millennials and Their Stuff in the Basement

Love is patient, love is kind.

1 Corinthians 13:4

Perhaps it's because our children all majored in art that, although they have flown the coop, our basement and garage still contain many of their belongings. One glance into the belly of our home belies the notion that the next generation is known to desire simplicity and fewer things than their parents. "*Really?*" we mutter as we strain our backs and occasionally stub our toes while shifting boxes of books, a drum set, random pieces of furniture, tools, canvases; and even an anvil and forge. As we sort through our own goods in an attempt to pare down, we realize we're caught in an interim season with our dear millennials and their stuff. They are out of the nest, but they aren't completely settled in homes that could contain the trappings of their various interests.

Apparently this is a common tale. I hear similar groans from other empty-nest parents who'd like to set their children's possessions on the curb. Years ago, I remember my own parents hauling my old schoolbooks, papers, and crates of odd items from my childhood bedroom to our honeymoon apartment when they needed to reclaim space in the house. It was only fair that they enjoy more of *their* home after the children moved out. They generously shared it with four kids long enough.

But thirty years ago, our generation tended to get jobs and more permanent places to live at a younger age than grown children do today. So we are digging deep for patience with our three creative kiddos. Every time the children come home, we ask them to eliminate whatever books, art supplies, and clothing they no longer need. Once in a while I remind them of our friends who told their midtwenty-year-old sons that they planned to sell the family home and move into a condo in four months. "Guys, you have until then to get your stuff. We aren't able to hold onto it any longer." Those young men got busy, knowing Mom and Dad meant business.

On the polar end of the spectrum, I know parents whose children's bedrooms haven't changed since the day the kids graduated high school. Those rooms remain memorials to their former inhabitants for the next twenty years. In my opinion, that is patience to a fault. Or more likely, it is Mom or Dad clinging unhealthfully to remnants of the past, almost pretending that the kids still reside at home.

For now, my husband and I are taking the middle road, encouraging organization and accurate labeling so everyone knows what is in the boxes that remain. We also keep our "empty the basement" mantra. In other words, Mom and Dad's house can't be a storage unit forever. Perhaps we'll accommodate their stuff until the educations are complete, but we hope the graduate programs don't drag on too long.

How ironic that as empty-nest parents push to declutter and downsize, many of our elderly parents are simultaneously singing the same song. And they need our help with the decluttering process. Yikes! Suddenly, the sandwich generation, you and I, must deal with our own possessions as well as those belonging to our children and even our parents. Many folks in the latter generation grew up during the Great Depression, and you know what that means—they didn't throw away much.

When my sister and I emptied my parents' home of nearly fifty years, we pored over photographs, letters, scrapbooks, linens, china, glassware, art, and furniture. We handled five generations of goods. It is a heartrending experience to catch glimpses of our great-grandparents' lives and to see images of our own grandparents, whom we knew well, in their younger years. It is an exercise in perspective. We see ourselves as dots on a continuum of ancestors and descendants. We are familiar with family members as far back as three generations. But forefathers and mothers prior to about 1825 are just names on a paper. This begs the question, in how many years will we be the same for our offspring's offspring's offspring? And how important is our stuff, anyway?

It seems that however valuable we think some of our things are, they're still just *things*. The stuff we hang on to is vulnerable to rust, moth, and thief. Don't get me wrong—I am not suggesting we toss every family heirloom. I treasure a spoon that bears great-grandparents' initials, and our daughter wears mittens that were knit by her great-great-grandmother, who was born at the close of the Civil War. But much of the junk that crowds our basement is a burden.

I recently overheard a neighbor (who has a very tidy home) talk with another mom on the block who complained about bins of her children's outgrown toys that she couldn't bring herself to jettison. Neatnik Karen wisely responded, "Your kids are not *in* the Playmobil! Pick a couple of special things, if you have room, and get rid of the rest!"

For us it's the Legos. They had a lot to do with the way our kids' minds function today. One of our boys even has Legos in the laboratory where he works, and sometimes when the children are home, they haul up the bin and engineer amazing creations as if they were nine years old once again. It is childhood fun revisited!

But as for extra stuff, it's time to say goodbye. We think we own our personal effects, but as they accumulate, eventually they own us. So let's lighten our loads. Let's also take an example from millennials, whose perspective on collecting things is generally different from the three generations their senior, who keep trying to hand them stuff. Stay tuned…

25

Millennials: What We Learn from Their Thoughts on Things

Do not store up for yourselves treasures on earth, where moths and vermin destroy, and where thieves break in and steal. But store up for yourselves treasures in heaven, where moths and vermin do not destroy, and where thieves do not break in and steal. For where your treasure is, there your heart will be also.

MATTHEW 6:19-21

For years our children learned much about the world from us, their parents. But as millennials have come of age, a natural turning of the tables is underway. Let us take a deeper look at the differences between the way baby boomers, Gen Xers, and millennials consider the accumulation of things.

As I mentioned earlier, many of the baby boomers' and Gen Xers' parents grew up during the Depression. When the lean years of their childhood came to an end, many wrapped their identity around possessions. They had gone without for long enough, and as they entered adulthood and established households, certain domestic goods communicated social acceptance. What kind of silver did they collect? Was it sterling or silver plate? How about their china, crystal, linens, and the china cabinet to house the goods? Starter homes gave way to larger homes, and as humans tend to fill whatever space they are given, boomers amassed a plethora of collectibles. The hunt for antique pottery crocks, rocking chairs, and lace tablecloths was recreation for many of our mothers in the 1980s.[1]

Fast-forward thirty or forty years, and the time has come for traditionalists (our parents), baby boomers, and Gen Xers (us) to downsize. And as we do, it is as natural as breathing for us to offer furniture, dishes, precious antiques, and what we consider heirlooms to millennial offspring who are setting up homes of their own. But millennials are wired differently. Many are kindly but firmly saying "No, thank you." This seemingly unappreciative response can lead to hurt feelings for parents who have held on to precious items, just waiting to gift them to children as a kind of legacy.

But many millennials (62 percent) are choosing to live in urban settings in fewer square feet than the suburban homes where they were raised.[2] They are confident in the aesthetic they wish to create, and Mom and Dad's brown furniture probably doesn't fit the picture. They're an adventurous bunch who would rather spend money on travel than on stuff, and their collections are digital—photos and videos of their latest escapades abroad.[3]

Some millennials embrace the tiny-house movement, choosing to live in 250 square feet or less, though the romance of this sort of shoebox abode often fails miserably when a little one arrives. There's simply not enough room for Mom, Dad, a baby, and their gear. Also, parents of tiny-house dwellers may well be the ones with too many boxes of their children's belongings in the attic or basement, proving that the tiny house is a bit too tiny after all.

But before we get our panties in a twist over our dear millennials who don't want our cherished stuff, let's consider what we can learn from them.

First of all, Jesus Himself preached that we are to travel light on this earthly journey.

> Don't hoard treasure down here where it gets eaten by moths and corroded by rust or—worse!—stolen by burglars. Stockpile treasure in heaven, where it's safe from moth and rust and burglars. It's obvious, isn't it? The place where your treasure is, is the place you will most want to be, and end up being (Matthew 6:19-21 MSG).

I'm not suggesting that millennials arrive at their sophisticated, clutter-free style because of biblical teaching. A few, perhaps. But for whatever reason they desire to live with fewer things, their idealism happens to resonate with this truth from the book of Matthew. Their wish to have goods that don't require time-consuming maintenance also supports the thought that time is a commodity not to be squandered. Millennials would rather spend quality time with friends, work hard, and play hard, using what time they have to the best advantage. Polishing silver and furniture is rarely a priority.

Those of us who are boomers and Gen Xers might even feel a tad envious of this fresh way of thinking. I accepted family treasures to honor the feelings of grandparents. As a result, we have too many things. Some of them I've held on to for the next generation. But now I see they may be bound for the donation pile.

Recently, a friend in my close circle of confidantes shared with us that she and her sister donated their parents' eighteen perfect place settings of Haviland Limoges formal china to the Salvation Army. The rest of us gasped in shock. But it was no longer useful to those who inherited it. I love their attitude that hopes someone who really needs dishes will walk into the secondhand store and be thrilled. Our friend said, "Even if it's a college student looking for plates and cups for their apartment, let the dishes be used rather than sit collecting dust at our house." Or worse yet, take up room in a storage unit, where they are inaccessible and an expensive, emotional burden.

In Sweden, a country replete with extraordinarily beautiful housewares crafted of glass, china, linen, copper, wood, and stone, there is a common practice called *döstädning*. While it may sound morbid, it is the practice of "death cleaning," which accurately portrays that part of Swedish culture where no one wants to bother anyone else. As a generation draws closer to the end of life, or to downsizing, Swedes do not wish to burden the next generation with their stuff. So, they intentionally clean and pare down.[4]

While traveling in Sweden, my husband and I observed the results of *döstädning* as we visited Swedish secondhand stores the country over. These curated shops are second to none. We were tempted by these treasure troves until we remembered that our house is full and our millennials are probably not interested, unless we happen to find a little birch basket that is congruous with their specific aesthetic niche.

Let's not leave a legacy of stuff to exhaust and frustrate our children. Rather, let's remember what holds lasting importance—relationships, meaningful experiences with others, and shared love. A relational legacy will last and be a blessing to upcoming generations. I would rather be remembered by a heart of gold than a sterling silver bowl.

26

Apple Pie at Midnight

*Above all, love each other deeply, because love
covers over a multitude of sins. Offer hospitality
to one another without grumbling.*

1 PETER 4:8-9

When I was a young mother, my friends and I admired Diana, Princess of Wales (as did much of the world). We pored over photos of her royal wedding to Prince Charles and later of their sons, Princes William and Harry. Diana's beauty, her grace, and her work with humanitarian issues impressed us, but as the fairy-tale marriage unraveled, we noticed the strained smiles and tears that betrayed her discontent. However, amid the tragic photos, there was one of pure, unabashed joy. It sticks with me. It shows an exuberant Diana with arms outstretched, bending to welcome her sons, who were running into her joyous embrace as they returned home from boarding school. It could have been titled, "This Mother's Greatest Joy!"

I agree with Diana. The best view from the front door of our empty nest is the sight of our children arriving home for a visit. Before the much-awaited day, we bake a fresh batch of granola to replenish the jar on the kitchen counter and make sure the beds are ready with fresh linens. Since our daughter is the only child who owns a car, she drives home and the boys fly. When I hear the familiar rattle of Johanna's Subaru rounding the corner to our house, I run to welcome her, thanking God all the way that she is safely home.

When the boys return, we meet at the airport or train station. I adore going to pick them up. The excitement of spotting a Tall Tree emerging from the crowd sends my heart soaring. Instantly my mother-eyes assess if they look tired, if they need a haircut, or if the most recent barber went crazier than the last time they were shorn.

But sometimes I'm too busy with preparations at home to make the joyous trip to get them. The last time our children needed a lift, my hands were covered with pastry dough. Eric and Johanna went to collect the boys while I baked apple pie and lit candles in the house, on the front porch, and in lanterns that hang from trees along the driveway. I kept busy in the kitchen with one ear cocked for boots on the front steps. Although the boys coordinated their flights to economize on pick-ups, one was delayed, which is typical. But when they finally piled through the front door well after midnight, dropping their duffels in the hall, the apple pie was baked and ready, and all was completely well! Of course, they were exhausted after traveling all day, but we hugged and laughed and tucked into hot apple pie à la mode.

What delight to reunite as a family—five of us, or even six if our former exchange student, Isa, can fly in from Germany. No one knows us as deeply as we know each other. As we share a unique history, we are able to just "be," even in the absence of words. Like all families, we share a common background, whether it's as choppy as the ocean in a storm or peaceful as a sleeping puppy. We are united by layers of memories going back to the beginning of our life together. What a gift. It's one that I am most aware of when our children return to the nest.

When they come home, I can't wait to extend hospitality to them. I feel free to spoil them in silly ways, which they tolerate better the older they get. Yes, they are our children, but when they return as young adults, we think of them as honored guests. It's fun to bring coffee to wake them up, or maybe coffee and a cinnamon bun midmorning.

The actual welcome home is important too. We all remember one night when the boys were scheduled to come by train, but it was delayed. Johanna and I waited in the car by the train station for three hours, freezing cold in the wee hours of the morning with an irresponsible amount of gas in the tank. When we finally arrived at home after three in the morning, we made cocoa and sliced into a loaf of German *stollen*, a Christmas gift from my friend, an accomplished pastry chef. As the sky brightened, we fell into bed, happy with our little welcome-home party.

I used to wonder if I were the only person who held the departures and arrivals of loved ones as if they were fragile china cups. But a piece of music changed my mind. During high school, our son Karl-Jon worked hard to play Chopin's "Raindrop" Prelude in D-Flat Major on the piano. This beautiful piece tells the story of Chopin waiting for his lover and her two children to arrive home from a shopping trip during a turbulent storm. A repetitive note throughout the piece depicts the *drip, drip, drip* of the rain on Chopin's window, and a dramatic center section emphatically cries out with concern for their well-being. In the end, they arrive, and the melody resolves to a peaceful, calm homecoming.[1] This music runs through my head as I wait for the children to come home.

It tells me that surely I am not the first person to feel the way I do, scurrying with butterflies of excitement in my belly as I clean and cook hospitality into our home. It's time to light candles. Make their rooms look neat. Bake something...even the aroma of a simple box of brownies will send a message of welcome.

When they first arrive, I try not to place demands on them. I resist hounding them to make dentist appointments until everyone has had a good night's sleep. They usually turn up dog-tired. We want our children to remember that home is still a refuge, a place to refill and refuel, not to be badgered. Nowhere else are they so known; we want them to feel deep love and connection. In our mutual familiarity, it's easy to injure one another because we are aware of each other's tender places. So we try to go easy and be gentle with the weary travelers after they have come by taxi, airplane, train, bus, light-rail…or if they drive for hours to get home.

Their minds need time to transition. I watch them look around the house to see if anything has changed. Our home is not the house where our children grew up, but still many things are familiar, and they have all been back to live in it from time to time. It's nice when they can relax. A couch that is more comfortable than anything they have in their humble apartments invites them to grab a fleece and collapse. They find a fridge full of food and a washer and dryer that don't require a pile of quarters.

But what we hope they find most readily available at home are open hearts of parents who love and miss them, who can't wait to hear their laughter warming the house once again.

27

A Puppy, a Rabbit, and a Bear

*Praise be to the God and Father of our Lord Jesus
Christ, the Father of compassion and God of all
comfort, who comforts us in all our troubles.*

2 CORINTHIANS 1:3-4

They did it again—they melted my mother-heart into a puddle. This is what happens when the Tall Trees (more accurately, young men) return home for a visit, and before they leave, make their beds and place a vestige of childhood on the pillow. It's what they learned to do as little guys: Smooth the comforter over the pillow and set their favorite stuffed animal on top. For Bjorn's lower bunk, it's his Pound Puppy, and for Karl-Jon's top bunk, it's his Goodnight Moon Rabbit, forever wearing blue-and-white striped pajamas. Our daughter took her teddy bear with her when she moved out, so his worn fur and sweet face doesn't tug at my heartstrings from her bed. But her empty pillow looks forlorn.

Johanna, Bjorn, and Karl-Jon came home last weekend for

a friend's wedding. It was an unusual midsemester treat. We had time to share in person what was happening in each of our kids' lives. At the wedding, we were united in worship, in communion, in wishing the bride and groom our very best. As we strolled with our children from the beautiful church across a picturesque park to the reception, brilliant sunshine and tolling church bells heightened the mood and put tears in my eyes. We enjoyed a sumptuous dinner followed by cake and petit fours and goofy dancing in a hilarious mob of family on the dance floor. We took pictures, we laughed, and we feasted. Needless to say, it was the highlight of the season.

And the next day, the children left. Again. One by car, and two by air, leaving in their wake silent bedrooms that had returned to life for three short nights. While they were home, my husband and I fell asleep to their chatter. Siblings who are close have much to discuss among themselves, and some of it needs to happen without us. It's music to our ears to hear the steady buzz of their conversation down the hall, punctuated by occasional peals of laughter.

But with their speedy breezing in and out, it's difficult for me to keep up emotionally. One day after they have gone, I run into the boys' room to put something away, and the rabbit and puppy on the pillows take me by surprise. They get me every time. Those soft, well-loved pieces of our children's childhood, lovingly placed on the pillows, seem to say, "Mom, our hearts are here with you. We know you miss us, and part of us misses you too. But now we are off, attending to our own lives, while you are here with Dad. We love you, but we are no longer five, six, and seven."

I can't look at those sweet beds for many minutes, or I will cry. These bunk beds that my husband had to extend by several inches when the boys elongated, becoming the Tall Trees, remind me of when they were small and I was a much younger mother.

As a ninetysomething-year-old friend recently remarked, "We are all about thirty-five in our heads, while our bodies are much older." Aha! That's it! In my head, I'm about thirty-two, and the children are five, six, and seven. I remember well their inquisitive questions, their minds bursting with ideas like flowers opening wide to the sun. They bounded—little engines, running for joy just to blow off steam.

Why, after eight years since the last one left home, does my heart still need comfort? Why is it hard to believe they are grown up? None of our children are yet married, and I wonder…if they were, perhaps with thoughts of starting their own families, would my emotions even out?

Mothering requires such deep affection, flesh of my flesh, such close ties. My husband and I gave them life, and we would give our lives for them again. Thus the tearing, the loving, the aching that never seem to end. Nothing can stem the love we feel for them. What will comfort my soul?

We have all heard it said, "Once a mom, always a mom." This thought came home to me in a fresh way while visiting with a friend who is one hundred years old and very wise. Not only does she think clearly, she is up on the news and fashion, and she is a sharp dresser herself. Recently, she shared with me her concerns for her son, a wonderful man, who is facing a difficult challenge. As I listened, it struck me that her words could be the same that I might utter about my children. The only difference is she is one hundred and her son is in his mid-sixties. Her heart as a mother is unchanged by her advanced age or the age of her son. He is all grown up, with children and grandchildren of his own, and still his mom is concerned for his needs and prays about them many times each day. Once a mother, always a mother!

In light of that, it makes sense that feelings we have about our children now may seem similar to ones we had when the kids were just little pumpkins. We look at our twentysome-thing children; we see them as they are but also the way they were at five months, five years, fifteen years, and every age in between.

Each age has its advantages and sweet spots. When children are little, we get to snuggle, tell stories, and encourage creativity and imagination. During elementary school, we engage in all kinds of learning. We do our best to survive the ups and downs of adolescent years. And then our children leave to continue their growing up separate from us while we are left hoping we didn't leave too many holes in their preparation. And no matter where they land, we miss them.

When the kids were little, we knew where they were, and there was great comfort in that. But that is no longer our reality.

The comfort we now seek comes from Jesus, the source of all true comfort. The empty nest forces the issue.

This promise from 2 Corinthians 1:3-4, "Praise be to the God and Father of our Lord Jesus Christ, the Father of compassion and God of all comfort, who comforts us in all our troubles," says it so well. In the absence of our children, I will cling to this God-shaped comfort that surrounds my heart with warmth and love.

28

Flawed but Forgiven

Be kind and compassionate to one another, forgiving each other, just as in Christ, God forgave you.

EPHESIANS 4:32

As far as the east is from the west, so far has he removed our transgressions from us.

PSALM 103:12

In all close relationships, it's natural that we tread on each other's toes from time to time, inflicting pain. We don't mean to, but it happens. With so much of ourselves deeply invested, the parent-child relationship is no different. It's best to deal honestly with relational offenses and hurts as they crop up, or else they build, layer upon layer, into a Gibraltar of resentment that eventually turns to bitterness. Forgiveness is the way to break down this relational mountain, and it requires intentional effort.

I am no expert in the fine art of forgiveness. In fact, it is something I struggle to do as God would have me do it. To forgive an offense, I must drop my pride and humble myself to the point of pulling my bruised toes out from under the offender's boots and gently, figuratively, step into those boots to see what the situation looks like from their perspective. This is not easy, particularly when the offender is clearly wrong and I am right.

Tongue in cheek! If I am an empty-nest parent who makes the assumption I am always right and my child is the one who blunders, I stand high on a dangerous precipice from which I am bound to topple. Our children make mistakes, but so do we. I think it's best we begin here.

That said, as empty-nest mothers, let's consider the specific need to forgive children who have erred. Certainly, sometimes we are proud of our children and what they do, but other times we are not. With children far away from home, we don't know all the ways they go off the tracks. In fact, we may not be informed until something has reached a devastating level. When our children lived at home, we used to pray, "Lord, if they are in trouble, please let them be found out. Early." But this is less likely when they no longer live in the next bedroom.

As late-adolescents learn to function in a fully adult world, their mistakes have consequences greater than those of, say, their middle or high school years. Do you have a college student who misses a deadline or doesn't pay a bill on time? Or one who goes where they ought not go or does what they should not do with those who are a bad influence? And while they don't mean to be ignorant, one who doesn't thoroughly question the way classes are scheduled may wind up needing an extra semester of college to the tune of several thousand dollars. As parents, we cringe…and dig deep to forgive.

We also wince at the errors of "invincible youth." These happen to the über-optimistic young adult who doesn't build margin into their schedule. They are chronically unrealistic about what they can pack into a day, a habit that necessitates all-night study sessions that produce second-rate work and lead to getting run down and ill. Or they scare us by minimizing danger—putting too many people on the boat, driving too fast, or drinking too much.

Some parents have children who leave home and major entirely in computer games, partying, and playing Frisbee golf. But Mom and Dad may not be aware until a dean's office or job supervisor blows the whistle. At this point the way out looks steep.

In addition to cringing at a son or daughter's poor choices, empty-nest parents have high hopes and dreams for bright children. We exhaust resources of time and money, pouring oodles of energy into our child for a couple of decades at least. Sometimes, as in the case of my father-in-law, the efforts pay off. The purchase of his violin required great sacrifice for his parents, but it was a worthwhile investment because he played beautifully for many years to come. But not all parents who mortgaged the house for a valuable instrument are this fortunate.

We all make mistakes. Some are more calamitous than others. We have friends who repeatedly told their sons, "Don't ever land in the backseat of a squad car." When it happened, and one of the boys called home, his dad let him hire his own attorney as part of the lesson to be learned. "Makes a mother proud," his mom said with a sarcastic smile when the charges were paid up. She too had some forgiving to do.

Recently, a wise friend who struggled to forgive her daughter explained to me, "I've really noticed the impact of my sin on others as I am trying to parent with the merciful love I believe God loves us with. I know I'm supposed to forgive her when she messes up and love her in a way that makes her feel worthy of love, not like she has to earn it. But my gut response when the same junk happens over and over is, 'There you go again, screwing up.' I realize how I sometimes make it hard for her to move on when my attitude holds her to her past mistakes. It is a real eye-opener for me. It shapes the way I pray for transformation. When I feel that bitter anger of unforgiveness well up inside me, I go into our bathroom (the only private space in the house) and pray aloud, 'God, transform my heart, remove the poison of my bitterness, have mercy on me, and give me Your grace in this situation.' Or sometimes, all I can muster is, 'Change my heart, change my heart…'"

If we find ourselves furious with a child who has misstepped, may we be able to pause long enough to remember our own errors of early adulthood. How did we disappoint our parents or cause them to explode with anger? Perhaps their response was unfair. But maybe it was right on. If we think back, how do we wish our parents would have reacted? From this place, let's thoughtfully craft our response.

Our dear offspring may not live up to our expectations. They may not seem to understand all we have given up for their good. But when did we grasp the breadth of what our parents sacrificed for us?

It is incredibly important for us to forgive children who fail. This is not to say we condone sinful behavior. We may communicate our disappointment in their choice or our disapproval of it. But in love, we extend grace. We communicate unconditional love that covers a multitude of sin, just as Jesus does for us. By doing so, we begin the process of forgiveness.

But perhaps the most difficult pardon to eke out of the hurting heart of a mother is forgiveness of oneself. In the parent-child relationship, this is complex. When children fail, I hear parents ask, "What could I have done to prevent my son or daughter from doing this terrible thing?" Perhaps nothing at all. But even if there is something we wish we had done differently, we must realize that we too are flawed… and forgiven.

We don't hear the father of the prodigal son beating himself up. If he does, it is out of our earshot. Rather, his intent is on loving his son who has squandered his inheritance on wild living. Like Jesus, he welcomes his prodigal with a hug and a kiss and lets forgiveness shine through a great celebration.

In the mire of our mistakes, Christ loves us and wishes to give us a second, third, fourth, and thousandth chance to try again. Bit by bit, as we give our aching heart to God with a willingness to let Him shape us into a more forgiving person, we are making progress. And the beauty of forgiveness is that God removes our wrongdoings from us. "As the east is from the west, so far has he removed our transgressions from us." Alleluia!

29

Saying "I'm Sorry"

As God's chosen people, holy and dearly loved, clothe
yourselves with compassion, kindness, humility,
gentleness, and patience. Bear with each other
and forgive whatever grievances you may have
against one another. Forgive as the Lord forgave
you. And over all these virtues put on love, which
binds them all together in perfect unity.

COLOSSIANS 3:12-14

I know my transgressions,
and my sin is always before me.

PSALM 51:3

When pride comes then comes disgrace,
but with humility comes wisdom.

PROVERBS 11:2

When children are little, parents have the opportunity to expose them to all kinds of interesting subjects. Children are sponges ready to learn about nature, the arts, science, literature, and history. How we adored watching our children discover Mount Vernon and its gardens, the Smithsonian, libraries, zoos, trains, planes, many kinds of music, an inky cave, vast forests, orchards, mountains, museums, and most notably, the beach. We often took Sunday afternoon outings, and vacations took us farther afield. But wherever we went, and no matter what we hoped to see, some of their learning was in the realm of relational lessons rather than in a specific subject.

For example, preschool children must learn to get along when they ride in three car seats squeezed so tight to each other that the back doors of the car barely close. Each summer, this was our challenge as we drove for a long day that began before dawn in Washington, DC, and ended just before sunset on the western shore of Lake Michigan. I smile to remember those driving marathons that took thirteen hours (including a few stops). When we arrived at the beach house where our extended family waited, we were met with hugs and kisses and excitement to get to the beach.

But one year, a brother-sister squabble nearly prevented our joyous moment of reaching the waves before sunset. I don't remember the actual injury delivered, just that it could not be overlooked. And I'll never forget holding one of our little boys by his chubby legs (he was that young) on the seat of a wicker chair while my husband and I implored him to simply say, "I'm sorry." It was a battle of wills. With our own hearts breaking with love, we held him in place while he cried miserably, making his chest heave deep sobs. Between wails we explained that with a quick apology to his sister, he would be free and we would all rush to the beach.

I glanced at my watch and at the sky that was quickly turning orange. At the fifty-minute mark, I got in his face and said, "Say 'sah'!"

He repeated, "Sah."

Now, I begged, "Say 'ree'!"

"Ree," the pathetic child sobbed.

"Now, put them together. 'Sah-ree!'"

"Sah…" Sob. "…ree." Sob. "*Sorry.*" Alleluia! Instantly we set him free and hugged him for coming through with the most difficult apology of his childhood. And we raced to the beach with glee.

Through the years we have reflected on this memorable lesson that our whole family observed about the difficulty and yet the necessity of verbalizing an apology.

Obviously, our little guy does not sit in time-out by himself. We are all worthy of our moments in the wicker chair to work on an apology. Why is it so difficult for us to say we are sorry? Not one of us on earth is above making mistakes, so why do we fuss rather than fess up and get on with bounding joyfully into the waves?

Pride! It is about protecting ourselves, our reputation, our feelings. My husband tells me I'm not good at taking correction, and I have to agree. To know I have hurt the feelings of a family member makes me want to jump on my bike and ride for miles. I feel safe. On my bike, no one can confront me as the wind whips my face and somehow frees my mind. But eventually I must roll my trusty blue steed back into the garage, trudge into the house, and face my error.

To apologize is to admit we have done wrong. This is hard. It requires the laying aside of abominable pride long enough to think about the feelings of someone else.

As parents of young adult children, my husband and I found ourselves in the uncomfortable place of being told by one of our children how we had failed them during the high school and early college years. As in the case of our three-year-old who was out of line, I don't recall the exact charges laid against us, but I think it had to do with us not understanding our child's perspective. I just remember the accusation was leveled on a college break at the end of a meal, and we were caught off guard. What I do recall is that we needed to offer a sincere apology, which was hard to do. Though that was years ago, perhaps we still need to go back to that thoughtful family member and ask if we truly said we were sorry in a way that was thoroughly meaningful.

Our child's honesty taught me that sometimes we are completely unaware of the ways we hurt others. In our humanity, we fall short. In our neediness, we miss what those closest to us need most, as we had done in this case.

A sincere apology is never followed by an excuse or throwing someone else under the bus. To say, "I am sorry, *but…*" and give a reason to justify behavior or to deflect blame is not a true expression of regret. It is not an apology after all; it is a defender of pride. Defensiveness immediately shuts down the potentially therapeutic conversation.

Rather, when we remember that humility rather than pride draws others to ourselves, we encourage relationships to grow. Even within our families, or perhaps especially within families, it is good to be open about our shortcomings. When we can lay down self-protection long enough to say we are sorry, goodness grows between us.

Madeleine L'Engle, in her book *The Irrational Season,* states it like this:

> It is not popular to be willing to admit to sin. The churches are still deleting *miserable offenders* from the general confession. There appears to be a general misconception that if we admit to sin, then we are wallowing in it, like hippopotamuses in mud. Maybe some people are. But freedom and lightness follow when I say, "I'm sorry" and am forgiven.[1]

And so it was for us. On a bright sunny Saturday, when my husband and I were called to account for being less than perfect parents, and we painfully agreed and apologized, a freedom and lightness followed that made the uncomfortable conversation worthwhile.

Our sin is ever before us. Have mercy on us, Lord!

30

Turtles, Tables, and Satellite Moms

*Be joyful in hope, patient in affliction, faithful
in prayer. Share with the Lord's people
who are in need. Practice hospitality.*

ROMANS 12:12-13

Turtles. We see plenty of them soaking up the sun on fallen trees over ponds along our bike trail. In early summer, I'm excited to spy seven or eight painted turtles lined up on logs, because they remind me of my special group of girlfriends from college. We call ourselves the Turtles. It all began when a bunch of us spent an annual weekend at the home of Lora's parents in Turtle Township, Wisconsin. Every February, the Turtle Township Firemen's Pancake Feed became the impetus for a relaxing weekend away from school in Chicago.

What a delightful time we had as the firemen gave us plenty of pancakes and attention. Lora's dad, Pete, was a volunteer fireman; as Pete's girls, we never went away hungry. But the long tables in the firehouse weren't the only place where we felt spoiled.

Lora's mom, Julie, served us generously the rest of the weekend at their bountiful dining table. Oh, how we girls ate up the love of a mom who wasn't our own mother. We made ourselves at home, lying all over comfy couches and easy chairs in halfhearted attempts at studying while Julie nurtured us in a no-nonsense kind of way. She encouraged us with sage advice, laughed at our jokes, and heard our stories about guys and capers in the dorm. She was the quintessential satellite mom, offering warm hospitality and love to the Turtles in midwinter, when we needed it most. How important Pete and Julie's example of welcome was. It was truly a gift to be in their home.

Now fast-forward thirty years. It is my turn to welcome the friends our children invite home. When they come, I think of Julie and the way she rolled out the red carpet for us girls. She makes me want to grab the extra-large stockpot and big mixing bowls to prepare mass quantities of chili, salad, breads, and brownies.

When our children arrive with friends, it is a double bonus. We are happy to be with our kids, but we are also thrilled to meet their compadres. As satellite parents, we get to love these young adult guests who miss their own moms and dads. We are privileged to listen and even offer suggestions that might be better received from someone who is not their parent.

I think of our daughter's friend Allie. How delighted we are when she comes to hang out at our house. Her mom and dad live far away, and she understands that our house is her home away from home. She may get milk from the fridge whenever she pleases and claim her seat in everyone's favorite corner of the couch, like any of our kiddos. She jokes that we throw elbows for that spot, which is partly why I take my turn before the light of day. When one of our children invites a friend to stay, they know they are inviting them to enjoy room and board. It doesn't matter what's on the menu; what matters most is the fellowship.

It is a bit unique that we have two identical tabletops in our family room. One is a well-worn pine oval-shaped table where we gather to eat, and the other is a replica of that tabletop, fastened to the wall above the couch. It's the backdrop for twenty-six small blue canvases. For our daughter's senior art project, she painted an item on each little canvas as it appeared in our former house in Kansas. There's a red teapot, my husband's guitar, a candelabra, my sewing machine, and a cream pitcher, to name a few. Johanna's art depicts our table as the center of community in our home. These unassuming domestic items are familiar and homey. Painting pictures of them and placing them on the "table" was her creative way of processing the upheaval of losing what had been her childhood abode when we moved.

Her piece conveys the coziness of home and the value of sitting down to share regular family meals around the table. Sometimes, though less frequently now, we still jam together, shoulder to shoulder, bumping knees with children and guests, laughing and finding nourishment in the provisions and the company.

More often, however, in the era of the empty nest, it is just Eric and me, leaning in toward a couple of candles at our end of the table, looking down at the empty side that formerly rang with laughter and the commotion of children and their friends clattering silverware and cracking jokes. Still, even for the two of us, the table remains an important place for conversation and connection. It is where we focus on each other and catch up on the happenings of the day.

The vacant side brings our thoughts back to satellite parenting. I can't say enough good things about adolescents and young adults who have the benefit of a relationship with grown-ups who aren't their parents. It would be preposterous to think that our own God-given moms or dads are the only ones who can help us find our way in the world. What a great benefit it was for me to hear the perspective of other adults like Pete and Julie when I was in my twenties. And today, I love to be in relationships with twentysomethings who could grow stronger in the glow of encouraging words from a caring friend who is the age of their parents. I might even make the same suggestion as their mother would—but without any friction of the parent-child relationship.

Sitting down to a meal with the Turtles, where Pete and Julie showed such care and concern for their daughter's friends, reminds me that it is my responsibility to put Paul's words in Romans into action. Even if I think a weekend is too busy and we are running out of extra beds or chairs, it behooves us to welcome guests at our table.

"Be joyful in hope, patient in affliction, faithful in prayer. Share with the Lord's people who are in need. Practice hospitality" (Romans 12:12-13). I can't think of a better place than at our table to offer words of hope, share faith as we pray, and be friends with our satellite children who need the warmth of hospitality.

31

Safety in Numbers

Carry each other's burdens,
and in this way you will fulfill the law of Christ.

GALATIANS 6:2

Rejoice with those who rejoice;
mourn with those who mourn.

ROMANS 12:15

By the time we reach the stage of the empty nest, it is likely we have gathered a covey of friends with whom we've shared various chapters of mothering. Years ago (which seems like yesterday), we toted babies in strollers and backpacks, often on outings with other moms and babes. It was natural. We birds of similarly exhausted feathers flocked together, holding each other up through MOPS groups, in our neighborhood Moms in Touch gatherings, and along the sidelines at soccer matches. Together we took our preschoolers to swimming and ballet lessons and taught each other's children at vacation Bible school. For me, these are happy memories.

Friendships with other parents were a good part of the

parenting journey, and they grew with us as the kids got older. During the school years, children were the connecting point with other moms and dads. Life was relationally rich when we had three students at our local high school. With activities to attend and places where we could pitch in, we got to rub shoulders with other parents, giving and receiving support as we served pasta dinners for the cross-country team, stitched costumes for musicals, and attended games and art openings.

Even at church, our small group formed largely because our collective gaggle of children were friends. Several families took turns meeting in each other's homes to share a meal and to pray with each other. It didn't take too many gatherings to realize that most of our praying revolved around our common greatest challenge, that of parenting. Frequently we admitted our parental blunders, laying our guilt out on the table along with dessert and coffee. We felt like a pathetic bunch of mothers and fathers and dubbed ourselves the WWPs (World's Worst Parents). Our kids knew it too. While the sixteen of them were zipping around together on bikes and skateboards or shooting hoops, we adults remained at the table, holding them up in prayer. As the verse in Galatians recommended, we carried each other's burdens in an effort to be decent moms and dads. Out of these gatherings, friendships deepened, and our children gained satellite parents—other moms and dads to care for them.

But now, in our empty nest, the organic getting together with other parents who know our children happens less frequently. For us, it's partly the result of moving, but I believe it is also because there are fewer built-in social connectors with other parents. We don't bump into each other at athletic or art events at school.

But even in this phase of life when we don't engage with other parents through kids' activities, relationships with other moms and dads remain vitally important. As an empty-nest mom, I still need a network of friends who understand the ups and downs of parenting at this stage of the game. Perhaps we don't perceive the need as readily as when we had a newborn and craved adult interaction. But we still benefit greatly from mutual giving and receiving of support as parents.

We are not meant to soldier on in a solitary struggle. But all too often this is the case.

One reason for this is that we fear being found out as a failure of a mother. It was easy to admit that a baby had a problem. Their issues were ear infections, pink eye, or colic. Babies are entirely innocent. Mothers of newborns are pretty close. But to tell a friend that a college kid is on probation or struggles with an eating disorder feels risky. It leaves room for judgment. So we tend to clam up in favor of self-preservation. Or is it preservation of our reputation and pride?

How important is it for us mothers of young-adult children to keep all our struggles sealed safely inside? To some extent, guarding the reputation of a child and in turn ourselves makes sense. But if we keep all our children's troubles and the resulting turmoil to ourselves, hidden from view, does this really promote self-preservation? This seems more like a quarantine, which is inherently lonely.

Naturally, this is a highly personal question that each of us must answer in a way that feels right for us. It would be unwise to advertise all our flubs and failures—or our children's. However, it is a godsend to have a trustworthy friend who listens well without speculating about where we or our offspring slipped up.

What a blessing and comfort to have a close friend who genuinely cares and will pray for us or our children at the drop of a hat. This is the kind of confidante who will jump up and down with us in moments of success. They will also cry genuine tears of sorrow when we are in pain. None of us are meant to travel the parenting road alone. The way is far too dangerous, the route circuitous. Sometimes it is scary and dark, and the landmarks are obscured and confusing.

When I was about eight, my sister and I were allowed to walk six blocks to buy penny candy on a busy street. Our mother told us, "Stick together; safety in numbers!"

Even if that number is two or three, we are better together than alone. This is why I still keep in touch with several friends who have known our children since they were knee-high to a grasshopper. We care about each other's children, and we care about each other—mother-friends still striving to mother well.

If my son lands a gyrocopter on the White House lawn, my friend Shelley will hear about it from me before she hears about it on the news. (By the way, that was *not* my kid, but it *was* some mother's son, and that woman needs a friend.)

Okay, that is a drastic case, but you get the point. As our children age, the types of scrapes they get into carry heavier consequences than when they were little. There are myriad more ways for them to shine or fail, galvanizing a mother's need for true-blue friends.

Many times, what makes this tough is our transient society. When we move, it's a challenge to stay close with friends and even family members whose children we have known and loved since birth. Few people stay put. We have nieces and nephews strewn from Alaska to California to Massachusetts. Keeping in touch requires effort. And since we never had the luxury of family living close by, some friends who became family for us are also on the list of those we greatly miss.

But whatever our situation, may the truth of Galatians 6:2 and Romans 12:15 be our reality. For my friend Shelley and me, maintaining a relationship in which we bear each other's burdens keeps the postal service between her house and mine unusually busy. For years since we both left the Washington, DC, area, we have "visited" every few days via snail mail. Shelley's letters keep me up on her children, who have been dear to me since they were toddlers or newborns. We haven't been neighbors for twenty-one years, but with well over five thousand letters that have passed between us, we do not mother alone. Far from it; we have the privilege of cheering, crying, praying, and loving each other and each other's children. While I wish my friend still lived around the corner, and many others whom I miss as well, we continue to offer support, not just as mutual back scratchers, but as friends who listen well, ask good questions, and pray.

None of us is strong enough or smart enough or brave enough to do the big task of mothering by ourselves. My mother didn't let my sister or me venture to 95th Street for penny candy alone, but together we managed. Similarly, I couldn't be an empty-nest mom without friends like Shelley, who understand.

32

A Cacophony of Quiet

He said, "Go out and stand on the mountain before the Lord, For the Lord is about to pass by." Then a great and powerful wind tore the mountains apart and shattered the rocks before the Lord, but the Lord was not in the wind. After the wind there was an earthquake, but the Lord was not in the earthquake. After the earthquake came a fire, but the Lord was not in the fire. And after the fire came a gentle whisper. When Elijah heard it, he pulled his cloak over his face and went out and stood at the mouth of the cave. Then a voice said to him, "What are you doing here, Elijah?"

1 Kings 19:11-13

Elijah heard the sound of sheer silence. How extraordinary! What does that kind of silence sound like anyhow? The absence of noise, I suppose.

This season in particular, I appreciate Sunday mornings in our little neck of the woods because it is quieter than the other six days. Construction trucks a quarter mile away turn a beautiful golf course into a bunch of boring houses, and they are loud. But the progress grinds to a halt on Saturday after-noon and doesn't resume until Monday morning. No back-up beeps, no rumbling of earthmovers. Just quiet. Though not everyone in our little community thinks about it, Sabbath is observed in the serenity of Sundays, connecting us to the week when God created the world. My shoulders relax. I exhale. On Sunday mornings, little sounds of nature are noticeable. Chip-munks and squirrels scamper. The birds sing their songs in harmony with the crickets. A breeze caresses the trees.

The quiet is so heavenly, I joke that I'll drain the gas out of any lawn mower or leaf blower that dares break the peace. It is what we need, what our souls crave, if we manage to stop long enough to realize it.

I don't understand the need for noise, only the desire for quiet. Noise is the given. It's what we get all day long. Whether it's traffic, trains, phones, conversations, music (I love music, but not *all* the time), leaf blowers, lawn mowers, or chain-saws. Perhaps you can't sleep without a noise machine. Not me; my soul craves what Elijah received when he dared step out of the cave—a cacophony of quiet. And in that peaceful, windless silence comes the voice of God, asking Elijah what he is doing there.

Imagine having to answer to the God of the universe about our whereabouts. What would you say? What would I say? Would we be able to utter a word? Would we stammer in con-fusion as we fall to our knees?

This morning as I enjoyed some moments of silent solitude,

I reflected on what is so difficult about being an empty-nest mother. What makes me feel angst in this season when children are suddenly out on their own? It was in the quiet that I heard God say, "Bonnie, get on your knees."

"Oh, but Lord, this chair is so comfortable, and my coffee just reached the most drinkable temperature, and I want to stay wrapped in my fleece this chilly morning."

"Get on your knees. For Me. You do it when you *really* want My attention. Well, now I want yours."

Compared to Elijah's terrifying wind, the earthquake that split a mountain, and the fire that came near, how big of a deal is it for me to get out of my cozy chair and kneel before God in humility and love? I thought of a pastor whose mother literally wore out her knees because she was on them praying for her children for hours at a time, year after year. That did it. I took to the floor, facing my chair. And I said, "What, Lord? What do You want to tell me?"

And there it was. The silence surrounding me as it had Elijah…but it was not silent in my head. I guess that's why people need noise machines to sleep. They are not afraid of the dark, just the quiet. Because when our ears aren't filled with sounds, all the worries that sounds keep at bay come running at us, loud and persistent and chaotic.

For a moment, I say, let them come bang on the door of my head. Knock on my heart. Tear at the windows of my soul. I hear you out there, and I see you too, you scary faces of evil that threaten to undo the peace I claim in Christ. You are right,

I *do* fear for our children. I admit I am powerless to protect them in the ways we used to, with blankets, warm mittens, car seats, antibiotics, and life jackets. Now they are out there, more vulnerable than ever to decide for themselves if they'll wear a helmet or thumb a ride.

I put my head down on the edge of the chair, and God holds me gently. He tells me in the quiet why the empty nest feels uneasy. It's because as a mother, I can't intervene in the ways that I used to when the children were little. When youngsters strayed into the street, or tried out a bad word, or fibbed, or were not responsible with chores, we parents did something about it. That was our job in raising our children.

But now, all we can do is pray, love, and lead by example. I pray that we said enough and encouraged following Jesus enough when they were little, and that their faith flourishes today. I pray that they remember what they heard about God's love for them. I pray they take to heart that they are all precious in God's sight and that He holds their hands through every difficult class, relationship, and decision. I pray they find good friends in their schools and workplaces. I pray that other Christians will surround and be present to them. I pray that they will pick up God's Word and let it guide their thinking and their loving. I pray for their friends and for their safety. I pray and pray and pray and love them from my little noiseless spot.

Time flies by, and the internal anxieties that hammered loudly in my head have all been lifted to God. And the din is diminished. I think of the mother whose knees speak of thousands of prayers, and I want to send her a pillow so she may continue one of the most worthwhile endeavors of an empty-nest mom.

When at last I straighten up with greater peace in my heart than I have known for a long time, I am able to tell Jesus what I am doing here. I am loving our children the best I am able in this stage of mothering. And I thank Him for speaking to me in the calm and quiet.

33

Finding Fulfillment in the Emptiness

Let all that I am wait quietly before God,
for my hope is in him.
He alone is my rock and my salvation,
my fortress where I will never be shaken.
My victory and my honor come from God alone.
He is my refuge, a rock where no enemy can reach me.
O my people, trust in him at all times.
Pour out your heart to him,
for God is our refuge.

PSALM 62:5-8 NLT

I said to my husband over breakfast today that it would be easier to write a book about "sixty ways to love your children" than to encourage empty-nest mothers to walk closer with Jesus. It's just wimpy me whining about the challenge, the joyful challenge, of dealing with something as unseen as germs or the wind. But we see the results of both germs and wind; therefore we know they exist. The same is true with our heavenly Father.

Sometimes in our nest of a home, I notice the places of emptiness. Some of these are actually helpful. It's nice that the driveway is emptier—and the laundry room, and the shoe basket by the back door. Some closets are emptier, while a few heavy-laden bookshelves wait to be sorted through and emptied by bibliophile children.

But of course, empty places at the table and by a roaring fire on a Friday night draw out the melancholy in my soul. Where children and friends of children once cavorted, it is quiet.

With much emptiness surrounding me, I long to let Christ indwell a bigger place; I long to be closer to Him. I have said this before, but I don't want us to lose track of this idea. Empty-nest mothers have an unprecedented opportunity to grow deeper in faith.

As we learn to trust God more with every aspect of our lives, we glorify God. As Julian of Norwich learned though a vision God gave her, God made us, He loves us, and He will preserve us. As we look to His goodness, we are connected to His great love, which allows us true rest and happiness deep in our souls in a way that nothing else can accomplish. As Julian says, God will preserve us.[1] I'll take that a step further: He will preserve us as mothers.

I believe this means that our efforts to love our children are never for naught. We all know at least one mother who is so incredibly disillusioned with her children that she would like to turn her back on them. But instead, when a mother chooses to hold her floundering kids up to Christ and begs for God's goodness to flow over them, this mother is protected and preserved. God stays close and sustains her as she clings to Him.

In our earnest desire for children to adopt our values, plenty of mothers don't applaud the actions or attitudes of their children. Sometimes moms have to look a little harder to see their son or daughter's positive attributes. These children may not fulfill a parent's idea of success, yet there is God-given goodness in them, and God is not finished moving in their lives. He is still molding them for His good, as He is us. We need to place those lumps of clay in His hands and pray like crazy from the sidelines.

Whatever I tell God about my children, I need to remember that first of all, they are His children. He gave my husband and me the tremendous privilege of bringing them into the world and nurturing their hearts and minds despite all our errors and blindsides, but ultimately, they are His.

That knowledge needs to guide my thinking, my praying, my fretting, and my trusting more than it does. It is not up to me how children "turn out." Thank goodness! I am sure my mind looks far too narrowly at the ways God is involved in their lives. He sees a far bigger picture than I could ever see. I need to step back to get out of the way of Him shaping who they are. I will stay actively engaged in prayer. I will love them and even speak up and ask if they would like my opinion when big decisions come to the forefront. But I need not speak out of fear, saying, "I'm afraid you are going to... (whatever blunder I fear)." I need to trust that God holds them and will always have their best interest in mind. I will never hesitate in telling them that they remain in my prayers, and I will not hold back my loving care.

But we must resist judging their every move or word they speak. At their ages, it is best for us to pray that they will remember what they were taught when they were children at home rather than make a lot of corrections about small things such as wardrobe choices or even vocabulary. We all have specific concerns for the children we love. Mostly, we need to connect with God's goodness. When we can pour out our hearts to Him, God is our refuge.

34

Gurney Faith

*He said to me, "My grace is sufficient for you, for
my power is made perfect in weakness." Therefore
I will boast all the more gladly of my weaknesses,
so that Christ's power may rest upon me. That is
why, for Christ's sake, I delight in weaknesses, in
insults, in hardships, in persecutions, in difficulties.
For when I am weak, then I am strong.*

2 Corinthians 12:9-10

Brothers and sisters whose faith lights the way for others
are incredible gifts from God. For me, one such person
is my sister-in-law, Randi, whom I don't get to be with nearly
enough. Still, with several thousand miles between us, I always
know she is up to the task of interceding in prayer and also
doing research when we are stumped by anything from insom-
nia to finding a good herbal tea. How lucky for me that my
husband's brother married well, because Randi adds so much
vitality and love to our family.

But Randi's life has not been a smooth path health-wise,
nor in a previous marriage. Because of the difficulties she has

known, her perspective inspires me to hold tight to Jesus. In her words:

> I know that I'm a strong woman and that I've handled a lot of adversity. I used to pray for strength when I was weak and meditate on Scripture about it. I would read in Isaiah 40:31, "They shall mount up with wings as eagles, they shall run and not be weary, they shall walk and not be faint." But I found in these last two years I have become so overwhelmed and heavy laden that even the thought of having to mount up, run, or walk makes me crumble in tears. You know my tattoo says, "My faith is not a crutch; it's a gurney." This explains how I pray and focus my devotions when life is too hard. I imagine that God Himself is wheeling me safely on a gurney. He is carrying me. Instead of praying for strength when I'm weak, I just pray, "Carry me, God. I have nothing right now." When we are weak, He is strong, and will be glorified.

I want to shout, "Yes, sister!"

The emptier we are, the weaker we are, the more our Lord carries us. When I think of a gurney, I am immediately transported back to my years as a hospital nurse. We used gurneys to roll patients anyplace they needed to go, but only if they could not walk or sit in a wheelchair. The gurney is reserved for those who are completely helpless. No one *wants* to take the gurney ride. It means being wheeled, while lying down, in front of strangers who kindly avert their glance. One feels exposed, often prepped for surgery or just coming out of it. None of us look our best stretched out on a gurney under the garish lights of a hospital corridor or squeezed into an elevator. And if a gurney is needed, chances are we probably feel pretty crummy too.

But when one is too infirm or weak to travel any other way, what a relief to roll along, stretched out under the covers. If you find yourself in this position, ask for one of those heated blankets and take it as a hug from Jesus warming you from head to toe. If you desperately crave privacy, pull the blanket over your head, and everyone will think you are taking your final ride to the morgue at the furthest corner of the hospital basement. Sorry, twisted nurse humor coming through, but I noticed that when I was on such a mission, the gurney and I received a wide birth and loads of respect. You may smile silently under the covers, knowing you are in much better shape than it appears, but do not breathe deeply. It freaks people out. Joking aside, gurneys don't lie.

As my sis, Randi, knows, when we are helplessly lying flat, the Almighty arms hold us up. In our vast neediness, we are safe and loved. On the gurney, there's no pretending that everything is okay. This clever cart with wheels tells the truth. We are incapacitated and vulnerable; we need special help to get from point A to point B, and the gurney does the job. It is designed to keep us safe with handy side rails to prevent tumbling out. It has brakes and bumpers for safety, and clean linens and a pillow for comfort.

Randi's perspective hits the bull's-eye. Her faith in Jesus Christ, like a solid serviceable gurney, carries her when she is too weak to travel any other way. And she knows who is pushing the cart. It is her Lord.

I imagine her face tilted up from the pillow to lock eyes with Jesus, who knows where she needs to go. He has the trajectory of the stretcher in his hands, and Randi is able to trust she is secure. She rests in the knowledge of her driver's love and care for her. Whatever worries weigh heavily, they have been tied up in a plastic bag that says "Patient's Belongings" and is shoved under the cart until a day when she is strong enough to face them again. In the meantime, the strong arms of Jesus push her gurney, guiding the way. He carries her all right, and offers comfort and warmth. And she is able to close her eyes and rest deeply in His love.

For when she is weak, in Christ she is strong.

35

Search Me, God

Search me, God, and know my heart;
test me and know my anxious thoughts.
See if there is any offensive way in me,
and lead me in the way everlasting.

PSALM 139: 23-24

To literally live this part of Psalm 139 requires courage. To welcome God, who created me and knows everything about me, to peer into the depths of my heart; to pick through the anxious feelings that I hide even from myself…these things terrify me. To lay myself bare before Christ is truly an overwhelming idea. I want it, and I don't want it.

Yet as I believe God knows it all anyhow and has my best interest in mind, I am encouraged to come wobbling like a toddler into His presence. Little by little, I want to let Jesus uncover areas of my life that need work. His work. But this is a big task that requires me to first step out from behind protective boulders where I like to hide.

One such boulder is my attempt to keep an efficient schedule. In running around trying to accomplish much, it's a challenge to give Jesus my undivided attention. With or without children at home, our lives are full of appointments and deadlines. We have all kinds of obligations to meet at set times. You and I know the tyranny of an ever-important schedule that is packed full, ignoring the need for margin. My husband and I admonish each other when one of us realizes the insanity of a day's demands by simply teasing, "You're going to do that in *imaginary* time?"

And when I do sit down to read and pray, I can be tempted to slide down behind a boulder of nonreality that keeps me from facing my guilt, my lack of love, my difficulty to forgive, my critical spirit. It's peaceful to stay in the shade of my hiding place on the mossy side of my big rock. It's cozy, and I don't have to see my sinful heart blazing in the sunshine. I stick to Bible verses that are succinct and full of love, the ones that are giving and not demanding. The verses that don't probe with difficult questions. The ones that are quickly read and easily understood. Baby food that went through the blender. I don't have to chew. I can sip and run. Lucky for me, because I have many items to check off my list before bedtime.

But this is not *really* what I want. Not at all. What I really want to do is come from behind my great stone and climb on top of it, sit down with Jesus, and just be. Without children buzzing around, I find greater opportunity to deal with other relationships, including one that has festered with misunderstanding for years. It comes painfully into sharp focus in the bright light of day.

I picture scrambling on top of giant bunches of granite in northern Vermont, over water and between enormous trees of the Green Mountains. I imagine sitting cross-legged next to Jesus. It is just Him and me in the woods, and we are not in a hurry. The crazy part is that He is more than willing to pay attention to me. I pull my little ragged Bible from my pocket, open it to the end of Psalm 139, and ask what He thinks. He has so much patience and love, but He also means business about paying attention to the words in a way that makes my heart jumpy.

My guilt is pricked when He asks if I have extended grace in a relationship that requires a lot of it. Or did I inflict more pain by insisting only on the truth? How desperately the two must be presented together. Was I wrong, Lord, to state the facts of a situation, knowing they might seem offensive to another, because I am fed up with nonreality that keeps us from dealing honestly?

A thin veneer of sentimental love grows brittle as it covers deeply felt frustration and hurt between people. I refuse to polish the veneer. No, I want to scrape it off, knowing what a mess that will make, and rebuild from underneath. I want understanding—the kind that comes from listening to each other, to be the bedrock of this troubling relationship. The one I struggle to love desires saccharine sweetness of untruth rather than plain facts lined up on the table like children's building blocks in primary colors. I desire peace, grace, and truth. I want to take those blocks that have become stumbling blocks and examine them together. Red, yellow, and blue. I wish for my adversary to say what caused pain and subsequent retreat. I long for truth, grace, honesty, patience, gentleness, respect, and listening…that will lead to love. But I must accept the fact that this may not happen. But even in accepting this, I will not contribute to the lie that everything between us is okay.

Speaking truthfully with each other may seem like walking through fire, but it is far more refining and redemptive than dancing around the edges in a smoky haze where we can't see each other. This is where misunderstandings continue to fester and keep us apart.

I sigh deeply and dare to address my Savior. "Jesus, You know my feelings about this. Here they are, spread out on this rock for You to look at. As we sit on dry granite above water as turbulent as these relationships, I know I am safe to admit my sinfulness to You. I am sorry for how slow I am to forgive. Help me climb down from this place ready to let Your Holy Spirit lead and guide in every relationship. Help us learn to love each other better. Make me humble. Please give me Your grace, and help me love more generously. I cannot change those who will not stay in the conversation; I can only allow You to massage my aching heart with Your love until I am able to be gracious even where love is not returned."

36

Standing for Justice

What does the LORD require of you?
To act justly and to love mercy
and to walk humbly with your God.

MICAH 6:8

This is what the LORD Almighty said, "Administer true
justice; show mercy and compassion to one another."

ZECHARIAH 7:9

We live in a crazy, broken world, fractured by more catastrophes than we can comprehend. This year as a nation, we have watched in dismay, with our heads in our hands, the violence of hurricanes, floods, earthquakes, fires, uprisings of disgruntled people, nuclear threats, and uncovered sex scandals. We have witnessed the horror of mass shootings, even in a church. Communities have been ravaged, and even if it isn't our house that is reduced to ashes or flooded beyond repair, our security is shaken. We lament. We cry out. We pray for peace. "God," we plead, "have mercy on us, please."

We wonder, has the world always been this upside down, or has technology made us more immediately aware?

Yet for many of us, it's business as usual as we board airplanes and go to work just as we have always done. But with children far away from home, when incidents strike even remotely close to one of them, we text with shaking hands and pray for a quick reply.

This fall we've had too many close calls with our boys. With one son at school in Charlottesville, Virginia, and one who travels between Boston and New York for work, both Bjorn and Karl-Jon were on the front lines to witness hatred and violence that struck innocent people. They were too near the hot spots for any mother's comfort.

Just as the school year was getting underway, neo-Nazis and white supremacists poured into Charlottesville and onto the campus of the University of Virginia. Karl-Jon, who has a keen sense of justice, stood by and watched in horror as Ku Klux Klan members wielded torches, terrorizing students and locals with outspoken messages of vehement hatred. They came armed and ready to harm whomever got in their way.

In preparation for a rally by the alt-right that would oppose the removal of a Robert E. Lee statue, Karl-Jon trained to be a silent observer with a group of attorneys who seek to protect the rights of all individuals. However, the radical alt-right went far beyond saving a statue; they came to intimidate and overpower other citizens and especially minorities. When violent outbursts caused law enforcement to stop the demonstration, Karl-Jon and his friends walked quietly away from the center of the melee in downtown Charlottesville, grateful to be away from escalating clashes between protestors and counter-protestors. But not everyone was ready to simmer down. Suddenly a vehicle sped into the crowd twenty feet from our son, killing a young woman and injuring dozens. Karl-Jon saw bodies fly through the air and heard the screams of the terrorized crowd as people panicked and stampeded. One of his friends had both legs broken. All were wounded emotionally.

Karl-Jon texted that he was fine—just a pedestrian and car accident. As I flipped to the news on my phone, I knew he was making light of a much graver situation to keep his mama calm. Feeling far away and helpless, all I could do was pray over the terrible scene as it unfolded in the picturesque college town that was now seething in chaos.

During the days that followed, the news reports brought more pictures of unbelievable outbursts of hatred, much to our horror and shock. We also saw clergy walk in solidarity, preaching peace instead of antagonism, love in the face of violence. Prayers and the love of Christ were spoken loud and clear. Again we pray, Lord, have mercy on us!

Last week my mother-heart beat fearfully once again. While visiting with my father, news of a truck hitting a school bus and plowing through cyclists in New York City flashed across his TV screen. Dad, who knows Manhattan better than me, thought Bjorn's work took him further north along Broadway, but within minutes I received a text from our son saying he was close to the tragedy but he was fine. Once again...*whew*.

"O Lord," I cried out, "why do our boys have to be near the

violence?" And then I thought of my friends whose sons serve in the air force and the marines. They must be in a continual state of intercession.

While I am not crazy about our sons standing up for what is right, I am proud of their efforts to personally promote peace and justice. They have done better than me to stand by voiceless individuals who are marginalized and silenced by the rules of society. They have learned to be streetwise, and they are concerned about policies that are unfair. I believe they view the world much the way Jesus did when He walked the beggar-laden streets of the Middle East. Jesus paid attention to people of every walk of life. He extended love to rich tax collectors and to poor people alike. He reached out to the mentally ill, lame beggars, women, and lepers who were worth less than nothing in that society.

We are called to the same commitment to love all of humanity. But we forget all too easily the needy and the hungry and politely turn our backs on policies that ignore what is best for our world and its inhabitants. Even the words "human rights" may make us squirm.

I pray that I will be open to learn from the idealism of our children who are wired to care and even sacrifice personal comfort for the sake of others. Their actions speak louder than all the hollow words I have uttered about caring for the hungry, the poor, the downtrodden, and the abused in our world.

I pray that we will all renew our commitment to act justly,

to love mercy, and to walk humbly with our God. As our children take this verse seriously and literally, let us also pray for God's hand of protection to cover them and for each of us to promote His peace and love in every way we are able.

37

Writing Down the Empty Nest

Trust in the LORD with all your heart;
do not depend on your own understanding.
Seek his will in all you do,
and he will show you which path to take.

PROVERBS 3:5-6 NLT

To trust in the Lord with a whole heart, to seek His will in all we do, is a tall order. It involves dealing with the complexities of life in a way that is unique for each person. As empty-nest mothers, we labor to untangle a spaghetti bowl of emotions over releasing children and deciding where we might next invest our energy. We may slide in and out of seasons when we feel like we've made strides in handling grief, or guilt, or even moments of inexplicable happiness. But other times it seems as though we are whistling into the wind.

To adjust to an empty nest, or even to let one fledgling fly, leaves us with a heap of puzzling thoughts to process. I visualize the mess like an enormous pile of Legos poured out on the floor. Every Lego set our children ever played with (and that I used to waste my time separating) has been combined into one chaotic bin. When it is dumped out on, say, New Year's Day, it looks like a bunch of bits and pieces that have lost their meaning because they are disorganized helter-skelter on the rug. Tiny helmeted heads roll around with train tracks, swords, plain bricks, boat gunnels, propellers, wheels, flags, and flagons. To me it is a mess, but apparently the grown kids love it, because they crouch down, enthralled, ready to build as if they are suddenly seven once again.

This pile of pieces could be my empty-nest thoughts and emotions. They need sorting to make sense. The best way for me to do this is to write in a journal. Okay, I hear the groans from some of my friends who emphatically cry, "I don't journal!" Certainly, writing thoughts on sheets of paper that are bound together is not everyone's cup of tea. But who doesn't make a grocery list? Or write a string of bullet points to create an agenda for a meeting? If one is dead set against putting prose on a page, simply expressing thoughts bullet-point style could be a form of journaling. If I am pressed for time, that's exactly what I do.

I began writing and drawing in a journal when I was a teenager because I wanted to remember special events and meaningful sayings, such as the lyrics to a song or a quote that caught my attention. Gradually, journaling became a regular habit. Every few days I wrote what I was thinking about, be it a relationship, something from the news, a mind-boggling question from a class, or a reflection on a portion of Scripture or piece of music.

As a young mother, I attended a journaling workshop that cemented the idea that journal keeping is worthwhile. And I am not the only one who thinks so. Just today I walked into our doctor's office and noticed a video ad promoting the value of journaling. The ad claimed that journaling helps us handle anxiety healthfully. It allows us to deal with grief, stress, difficult relationships, and problem solving.[1] When I sit down to write, one sentence leads to the next. An idea builds upon the one before it. I never know exactly where the process might lead, but almost always it is to a place of greater peace and calm in my mind.

I pick up a few of those mental Legos and put them together in a way that makes more sense. Once they were jumbled and out of logical sequence, but now they begin to appear in a form that I comprehend in a fresh way.

Sometimes a journal entry is a feisty rant about an injustice that gets under my skin. I am worked up and angry, and my journal is a safe place to expound. Or after a misunderstanding, I am able to write clearly what I was not able to verbalize in the heat of the moment. And thank goodness, in my journal, I am free to name my fears rather than carefully tuck them under the floorboards.

Not only does journaling clarify thoughts, it helps us face painful emotions head-on. In other words, it helps us make sense of the grief we feel as children leave. I may be very happy with the newfound freedom of an empty nest, but sadness pops up now and again because I miss our children and the joyful commotion they brought into the house every day. When I write about it, I am surprised how instructive the process can be. It helps me think creatively about ways to channel the ache in my heart. As I write I'm pushed to action—to call a friend who also struggles with an empty nest or to send a message to one of the kiddos.

But perhaps the most wonderful aspect of keeping a journal is being able to write my prayers. When a journal becomes a collection of handwritten letters to God, I see His loving presence in all my concerns, joys, frustrations, questions, fears, and aspirations. He hears it all. And for some reason, once I transfer the jumble in my head to the pages of my journal, I am freer to go on and do what needs to be done. The *doing* is a result of *being* who God created me to be, and this emerges more clearly through written words or a simple line drawing.

One journal entry went like this:

> Why do I feel so tied to my journal to help me sort out my thoughts and questions? I guess I have to write to organize the confusing parts of life. God, You know I am not proud of the dinner party we hosted last night. I felt stressed, frustrated, and rushed. The food needed more love. As much as I wanted to focus on Your goodness, I noticed all kinds of little negative things going on around me. Pretending. Selfishness. I did not let Your

love shine through me as I had intended. God, I am sorry. I pictured myself doing better than I actually did. I am sorry.

By writing about an evening that was a disappointment for several reasons, I see my need to ask forgiveness, and an even greater need to forgive. My journal is the place to name these realities and constructively deal with them.

But the greatest blessing of keeping a journal is the occasional flipping back through pages from the past to see how God has intervened broadly and minutely, weaving His loving care into the fabric of my life. I don't look back very often, mostly because I am caught up in the present. But when I do, I am amazed to see the ways God directs the path of my life. I don't need to depend on my own understanding. That would be ludicrous. If my journal claims anything, it is that God *was* with me…He *is* with me…and I trust He *always will be* with me.

38

Because He Bends Down to Listen

I prayed to the LORD, and he answered me.
He freed me from all my fears.
Those who look to him for help will be radiant with joy;
no shadow of shame will darken their faces.

PSALM 34:4-5 NLT

I love the LORD because he hears my voice
and my prayer for mercy.
Because he bends down to listen,
I will pray as long as I have breath!

PSALM 116:1-2 NLT

A friend who enjoyed having a boomerang son back for a six-month internship has just watched her nest empty for the second time. She explains that when he first left for college, it was difficult, but eventually she adjusted. But this second leaving feels more final because the internship led to a first job, and it's likely this son will never live at home again. He has moved to a studio apartment in New York City where he barely knows anyone. My friend raises her cupped hands in front of her saying, "All I can do is hold him up to Jesus. I just lift him up, trusting that God knows all his needs. It is not always comfortable, but it is all I can do!"

When I think of our children in their faraway places, I imagine my arms stretching out to them as I pray. I picture their specific environments, the three we have visited and the one we have seen only in photographs—an architecture drafting studio and the funny old house where Karl-Jon's bedroom is a long, skinny sun porch with a lofted bed.

It used to be that I would naturally pray, "Be with Johanna, Bjorn, Karl-Jon, and Isa." But I don't pray that anymore because it goes against what I know about the omnipresence of God. I don't need to ask Him to *be with* our children. He is already there, wherever they are. Rather, it seems more appropriate to ask God to nudge our loved ones to sense His presence, to be touched by His warmth, to encounter His love in a new way. This slightly different angle of praying reminds me that as Christians, we need to actively respond to God and His loving care by noticing Him. That is what I hope for our children. It isn't God's style to push Himself forcefully on any of us, but through other people, nature, literature, music— even studies—God shows up, especially if eyes are tuned to be observant. So that is my prayer. Make them aware. Help our children mind the light around them that is the Spirit of God.

Going beyond praying for cognizance of God's presence, I pray that our children and their faith grow stronger through the challenges they bump into every day. While it is natural to hope our offspring will live with less discomfort and fewer struggles than we endured, it is better to hope our children will be equipped to handle whatever difficulties come their way.

So much is out of our reach. In my mind's eye, my arms reach to our boys in Massachusetts and Virginia, and to the girls in Michigan and Germany. And I see my friend holding her cupped her hands aloft, lifting up her son, the newcomer to New York. These postures of prayer mean we are handing children over to God. We care for them with every ounce of our being. At the same time, we realize that this phase of the emptying nest inclines us to deepen our experience of prayer.

Because of the distance between us and our children, they are very much on their own, and have been since each one left for college. While I have envied other parents whose kids attend in-state schools, the miles that separate us from our children provide great opportunity for cultivating faith. The kids are moving on to a new chapter of life, and as the parents, we enter a new phase of listening and talking with God.

One early morning before dawn, I brewed my typical pot of coffee and made a batch of granola before sitting down to my books and prayer. I read excerpts from Julian of Norwich's *Revelations of Divine Love* about an incredible encounter she had with God. When she was a young woman, she became deathly ill. While on what she thought was her deathbed, Julian saw a vision of the Trinity that filled her heart full of overwhelming joy. She was astonished that God would care to be intimate with a "sinful creature such as I."[1]

This is mind stretching for any of us when we consider the greatness of God compared to our own insignificance. As I considered Julian's ideas about this, also wondering how God could care for me, I noticed a curious crackling noise coming from the pans of granola cooling on the kitchen counter. I felt drawn to the little sounds and went to bend over the warm pans. As the granola wafted delicious steam into my face, I realized the noise came from hazelnuts hissing and popping as they cooled. With my book in hand, I returned to the couch to keep reading. As I settled back down, my eyes went to Julian's next paragraph. Its title was "No Bigger than a Hazelnut." Crazy coincidence? Rather, I believe it was God saying, "Yes, I am as present to you this morning as I was to Julian of Norwich in 1373."

It's a tiny thing, but as my heart crept deeper in prayer, I read about a hazelnut while hazelnuts (which I had never included in our granola before) crackled musically on the pan. I laughed, catching a glimpse of the joy-filled goodness that met Julian in her vision of a small ball in the palm of her hand, which she described as no bigger than a hazelnut. Because of its seeming insignificance, she expected it to disappear. But it did not go away. Rather, it gave her a strong message: "God made us. God loves us. God protects us."[2]

She also discovered that in focusing her prayers on God's goodness, she was filled to overflowing with a powerful sense of His grace and love.[3] Call me crazy, but God spoke to me through her words and through the unexpected crackles of papery hazelnut skins. God speaks in mysterious ways when we avail ourselves to His language.

Julian of Norwich, who lived during the time of the bubonic plague and great civil unrest, had faith enough to pen the saying "All shall be well, and all shall be well, and all manner of things shall be well."[4] She helps me see that praying for our children, while focusing on the goodness of God, is worth every minute I can devote to it. I may not have the luxury of praying and writing all day, because I need to do chores like bake granola, go to work, and do the laundry. But even in these activities, my prayers go on, reaching to far corners of the world on behalf of our children and the nieces and nephews we hold dear. They are covered by prayer, and I trust that God bends down to listen.

One final thought on prayer: Why not let the children know we pray for them? While they handle demanding schedules—busy worker bees in schools, laboratories, and libraries—the prayers of their parents cover them in the light of God's love. And part of our prayer is that they sense His warmth.

39

Letting Consequences Teach

*Commit to the LORD whatever you do,
and he will establish your plans.*

PROVERBS 16:3

*The LORD directs the steps of the godly.
He delights in every detail of their lives.
Though they stumble, they will not fall,
for the LORD holds them by the hand.*

PSALM 37:23-24 NLT

*He will feed his flock like a shepherd.
He will carry the lambs in his arms,
holding them close to his heart.
He will gently lead the mother sheep with her young.*

ISAIAH 40:11 NLT

Of all the experiences in my life, none has hammered home what it means to be a child of God as plainly as having children. First of all, consider what qualities our heavenly Father hopes to grow in each of us. He desires for us to expand our faith, to love more completely, to be honest and discerning, gentle and kind. He hopes we will gain the ability to forgive, to be empathetic, patient, and full of wisdom. He wants us to get along with our brothers and sisters.

Similarly, don't we also hope these wonderful attributes will shape the character of our children? But how do we impart these qualities on those in the next generation whom we love?

When children are little, we do our best to encourage kindness, self-control, honesty, and the ability to share. Our children's kindergarten teacher's first lesson was "Keep your hands, feet, and objects to yourself." Not bad habits to carry through life. But of course, there's more to "being good" than that. How about what comes out of our mouths, which is a reflection of what's stirring in our hearts? As parents, we do our best to bring up our children to be loving, respectful observers of the golden rule and the Ten Commandments, and to be good citizens. And like us, sometimes they fail, and we must redirect. Some goofs are small and unintentional. A forgotten assignment. A lost ID. Perhaps a speeding ticket. And some are more calculated—lying about their whereabouts, staying out past curfew, obfuscating the truth. As layers of responsibility mount, so do potential hazards.

As conscientious parents, we wish to spare our offspring impending consequences. But at some point, the mulligans run out and children must muddle through, learning important lessons on their own. Some years ago, it was the same for us. In fact, how many of these qualities do we still work hard to hone?

Naturally we wish to spare our children pains we have suffered, so we share the realities of our mistakes or point out the sad consequences of another's. Unfortunately, however, certain insights are best gained through experience. And as parents, sometimes the most loving thing we can do for our children is to allow the chips to fall where they may. In other words, let the mistake do the teaching. When this happens, we might have to bite our tongues until they bleed to keep from saying "I told you so."

How many of us grasped every concept by simply being *told* what is best or wise? As young adults, were we insightful enough to heed our parents' admonition, or did we have to feel the wind in our faces to wake us up to reality?

As we think about God as our heavenly Parent, do we recognize when He permits us to learn through our blunders? We don't focus on the right things, we waste time, we lose our tempers, we succumb to gossip, and we are taken in when we should have noticed a red flag. At times we fail to forgive, we forget to say thank you, and we miss the person next to us who needs our kindness. Yet God in His gracious way welcomes us back to Himself with the open arms of a loving parent.

The next time we feel completely frustrated with an eighteen- or twenty-six-year-old offspring who seems to ignore our excellent advice, let's stretch to realize that we might be in the same boat, frustrating God. He could be the Parent who is standing by, letting us learn at our own pace through the consequences of our errors.

When it comes to our children, oh, how we want to catch them, to cover for them, to spare them the trouble, the ticket, or the costly fine. But remember when they first learned to walk or ride a bike? Letting them fall was part of the process. Sometimes the results were bloodied knees and bumps on the head. We bandaged scrapes and restored their courage so they would try again, and in a sense, we do the same for children who are fresh out of the nest. Of course, the errors of today have heftier ramifications, but sometimes our kids need to arrive at solutions on their own.

It is a fine line between letting children fail and keeping their records clean. So we pray for insight. We know wonderful parents whose children were forced to navigate the legal system, only to land in jail. Others we know cautioned smart kids about their choice of a marriage partner, only to see that marriage end in divorce within months. This is hard stuff, and scars run deep. In such situations, it is difficult not to take on our children's pain. We suffer with them, hurting every bit as much or perhaps even more than the children themselves.

And isn't that what God does for us? With His enormous love, He cares for us and hopes to see us make good choices as well. As we gratefully receive grace, may we generously extend grace.

40

Ground the Helicopter

Have I not commanded you? Be strong and courageous.
Do not be afraid; do not be discouraged, for the
LORD your God will be with you wherever you go.

JOSHUA 1:9

I t requires an exorbitant amount of strength and courage to
parent and release children. When they are young, we strive
to give them strong roots to keep them grounded. As they
mature and prepare to vamoose, we hope we've built into
them what they need to fly in a world that doesn't cut many
breaks. When they first fly, it is natural to keep *some* tabs on
our children. Are they settling well into their new surround-
ings? Who are their newfound friends? How are finances holding out? How are their jobs, their bosses, their roommates, the
demands they face? Are they making the grade? Are they eating well?

But how many tabs are too many?

When our kids first land in a new place, I like an excuse to
call. "Do you need me to send your gray hoodie that was on
a hook by the back door?" All the while I'm hoping for news

about their fresh location, but I don't want to pry or pester. I may ask some of the aforementioned questions, but I don't want to give the impression that I'm afraid they can't survive without my assistance. Because I know they are able.

But out of the great love we have for our children, and sometimes out of our need to be needed, it is easy to cross the line from being helpful to over-involving ourselves in our children's lives. We may slip unintentionally into some level of helicopter parenting. As we long to see our children succeed in this world, what might seem like a surefire way to assist our children to the top might do the exact opposite. Let me explain.

When our children are little, we help them put on jackets and tie their shoes. But at some point, we must let them struggle to master these skills on their own. It takes more patience to wait for them to zip and go rather than help them. But we'd best wait, for it is the struggle itself that teaches.

Now let's skip ahead to more crucial skills. High schoolers write term papers, mind deadlines, fill out applications, prepare to interview, and make increasingly weighty decisions. If we hover like helicopters and swoop in to rescue our children from every failure and disappointment, we actually sabotage their confidence, resiliency, and self-esteem. If this becomes habitual, it often leads to anxiety and depression as students become fearful they won't make it on their own. This is why university counseling centers are flooded with students who deal with anxiety about failing at school. They suffer with underdeveloped coping skills and lack basic life skills, such as doing laundry and cooking. Many are children of parents who refuse to cut the apron strings.[1]

Helicopter parenting is a setup for trouble. The casualty is the child who needs to find success on their own. If we take on the responsibility for arranging classes, friendships, assignments, internships, and travel itineraries, we give the impression we think them incapable. The same happens if we mind critical decisions, deadlines, and job applications. Our overbearing presence cripples, which is the polar opposite of what we set out to accomplish.[2]

This is a practical challenge for any parent, and it is a spiritual challenge for parents who seek God's wisdom to parent well. Most of us are tempted to rescue a child in one way or another. Who has not at least once called in sick for a son or daughter who did not finish an assignment on time? Who has not rushed in to fight for our child in the face of an unfair grade when the student could learn to advocate for himself or herself? Which of us hasn't covered a bill or floated money when a child was irresponsible? And who hasn't wanted to give the boot to a boyfriend or girlfriend who broke our child's heart?

Obviously, there are times to protect our offspring. We do not let children play on the edge of the highway, and we don't look the other way in the face of abuse. But if we must be our child's best friend (which is known to prevent healthy relationships with peers), or if we insist on being included in every decision, we probably need to learn more about the dangers of helicopter parenting.[3]

Let's consider what pushes us parents to hover and rescue. Some of us have grown fearful in the wake of 9/11 and recent economic recessions. We feel the keen competition for acceptance into excellent universities and in the workplace. We see the squeeze on the middle class, and we are anxious, fearing downward mobility for our children. Perhaps some of us felt neglected by our own parents, and we overcompensate to make sure that won't be our child's story. We see other moms and dads over-parenting, and we feel pressured to do the same.[4]

I'm not blithely saying you should trust God and toss your high school graduates into the deep end to see if they can swim. Not at all. But disappointment is part of life. So is failure, and so are consequences for actions. We cannot prevent these so-called negatives from touching our children. In fact, it's best that the pain of bitter disappointment be felt while kids are still under our roofs. They are boats in dry dock, safely in the harbor of home. That's where their character is built, piece by piece. Sometimes in the building process, things go wrong. Our child is benched or earns a D in math. But they are at home, where it is okay to cry and stomp around in frustration. In their fury, they must decide what to do with the failure. As the harbormasters, parents may encourage and listen. Boards are ripped off and replaced. Eventually children graduate. Their ships are pushed out into deeper waters, where squalls send giant waves to buffet their boats, testing their strength. But their vessels were well built by disappointments weathered, failures faced head-on, and they will remain intact. Not only that, our precious children will know greater confidence that will serve them well when gale winds pound again.

In order for us moms to step away from parental helicopters, we may need to consider how and when we hover too close. Going even deeper, what motivates us to do so? Are we anxious about letting our children feel the wind in their face? Do we wince at their pain? Do we intervene out of fear of failure, either for them or us?

As parents, may we pray for wisdom. This is not easy stuff. Let us contemplate what work we need to do in order to ground those helicopters in our own backyards. Let's not hover to fulfill a need of our own; rather, let's try to do what is best for our children. Whenever possible, let's be strong and courageous, not afraid, and not discouraged. The Lord our God will be with them wherever they go. Let's hand our children the controls and let them experience the thrill of liftoff.

41

Till Death Do Us Part

*To Him who is able to do immeasurably more than all
we ask or imagine, according to his power that is at work
within us, to him be glory in the church and in Christ
Jesus throughout all generations, forever and ever! Amen.*

EPHESIANS 3:20-21

Transitions beg for recalibrations, and the empty-nest transition is no exception. Even before the fledglings fly, we brace ourselves and realize we are in for a jolt.

During a conversation with a mom who was contemplating the final stage of this imminent shift, I asked what would fill the void when the last of their three left for an out-of-state school. This mother has been extremely involved in her children's lives; in fact, she is the most devoted school volunteer I have ever encountered. My question didn't surprise her half as much as her reply startled me. I could tell she had given the empty nest considerable thought. She drew breath and said, "Well, one of my friends, when her last son finally left, went back to school. She earned the PhD she always wanted, divorced her husband, and started over."

Apparently I did a lousy job of concealing my horror, because she immediately tried to console me. "I think it's wonderful! My friend is happier than ever!"

Okay, it's not my place to judge. But I immediately thought of another friend, whose parents' divorce during our freshman year of college tore her to pieces. She could not hide the agony of her grief as her mom and dad, whom she thought were happy, dissolved the marriage.

We may choose to walk away from the marriage we know to find the happiness we think we deserve, but is this really best?

It's no wonder that our sage-of-a-psychiatrist friend reports that the bulk of the patients he counsels are middle-aged women who struggle after children leave home. He says they must come to terms with who they are. And if their marriage shook along fault lines when the children were at home, now it is quaking loudly.

When couples turn their focus toward children for twenty-something years, and suddenly those children aren't there, we have an important choice to make. Do we light candles on the table between us? Or do we snuff them out and walk away?

If we choose the latter, while the wick still glows with a red tip and a little column of smoke rises, I suggest we push our chairs in slowly, and as we do, look deeply into the face of the one we think of leaving. Hopefully this will buy a few moments to carefully consider our final decision before we toss a quarter century of history into the trash like worthless leftovers.

Of course, it's not always the mom who chooses to walk. Some husbands of the freshly emptied nest ask the difficult question, "Are we going to stay together?" And others don't ask at all; they just pack and leave.[1]

Many women feel they invested more time and relational energy with children than with their partner, and therefore they assume the agony of the empty nest is harder on them than on their husband. Whether this is true or not, each person must decide how they will face the empty nest, either constructively or destructively.

In the hustle of raising children, a husband and wife might become compatible roommates—good colleagues who do the work of child-rearing as effective business partners. Together they turn out successful and productive children, in whom they have poured the bulk of their interactions. When the children leave, it's natural to wonder, "What did we used to do BC (before children)?"

One thing we can all agree on is that this is a hard stage, just as having babies once was. But perhaps this is the best time to begin new activities together or rekindle ones that went by the wayside during the child-rearing years.

If only one of your kiddos has flown the coop, what would it mean to start investing in your marriage now? The emptying nest is a new phase but not necessarily a bad phase. Still, we need to make a conscious effort to feed the relationship. As the saying goes, the best time to plant a tree was twenty years ago. The second-best time is today. By investing in the marriage now, we prepare ahead so when the last one leaves, we may happily price a second honeymoon rather than a studio apartment.

When our children were little and they balked when we left them home with a babysitter, we said, "We will be a better mommy and daddy if we get to go on a date by ourselves." This has not changed. As we keep the vows made before the wee ones came to bless and challenge, God will bless our efforts.

As a friend of mine wisely asks, why would we think life could be better with someone else? This world does not believe in keeping promises. It calls to us to have as much thrill and fun as we can find. However, second marriages are statistically more fragile than firsts. In fact, first marriages have a fifty-fifty chance of surviving, but second marriages have a 67 percent chance of failing, and thirds rise to 73 percent. The major reason is most likely the lack of children and family relationships that can be the glue between husband and wife.[2]

If a marriage struggles, both parties must make a mental decision what to do with the relationship. As we act on that cognitive decision, our emotions follow. Since this is God's desire for His people (except where abuse abounds), He will strengthen us and do immeasurably more with our lives than we can even imagine. This rejuvenation will bless the next generation and the next after that.

In an affair, the thrill of a new romance may feel exciting. But as everyday life becomes routine, the mundane returns—with a structure more complicated than the lines drawn around the original family. Ask anyone who is part of a blended family at the holidays. Some challenges are gone, but new ones are created. The third and fourth generation is influenced, as it always is, but not necessarily in a positive way. These are hard words for some to read, and even harder to live. That is why we need God if we are to live the impossible, to hope where hope has given up, to believe that He is with us imagining deepening love between a husband and a wife who are much more than good roommates.

Ways to Strengthen a Marriage

- Dare to pray together. Start simple. A few words.
- Read the Bible together.
- Read books together.
- Remember what you did for fun before you were married.
- Learn something new together.
- Go out of your way to lovingly serve your spouse.
- Buy tickets to concerts and shows, and look forward to going…together!
- Talk about the most romantic time and place you experienced together. Revisit or replay it the best you can.

42

Identity Theft

> *Be content with what you have, for he has*
> *said, "I will never leave you nor forsake you."*
>
> HEBREWS 13:5 ESV

One of the greatest disappointments of our children's lives happened at the Nelson-Atkins Museum of Art in Kansas City, which is ironic because it was their favorite place to spend a Sunday afternoon. One day after church, we ate lunch in the museum's Roselle Court, a lofty enclosed space surrounded by arched colonnades with an authentic Roman bath spouting water in the center. As we sipped soup and shared scones, our seven-, eight-, and ten-year-olds noticed a banner announcing an exhibit of "Henry Moore's Working Models." My husband and I wanted to have a second cup of coffee, but the children were anxious to see what these working models were all about. They had visions of action, of interlocking gears that turned intricate parts with precision. Remembering my brother's model steam engine, I pictured steam rising and whistles blowing. We all imagined it differently, but in each one's head lay something magical and exciting.

The children begged that they might go together up to the gallery that was on a balcony overlooking the restaurant. We gave permission on the promise of good behavior, and they were off at a brisk pace. Eric and I enjoyed a leisurely second cup of coffee and wondered together what Henry Moore's working models could be.

Before we finished and went upstairs to join them, they rejoined us, looking glum and crestfallen. "What are these working models?" we earnestly asked.

"They're just little sculptures of people. Some of them have holes through them. They're dumb. They don't do anything but sit there."

Oh dear, such a letdown! We asked them to take us upstairs and show us these terribly uninteresting forms. To a certain extent, the children were right. In front of us sat seven or eight figures of reclining women who could not move. Most of them had exaggerated hips, softly rounded shoulders, and beautiful necks. We commiserated with our young artists and asked why they thought Henry Moore made these little sculptures. But it's hard to reengage disillusioned children.

Eventually we walked outdoors to the museum's sculpture garden and saw Henry Moore's larger-than-life human figures, which because of their size were more interesting. But still, no gears turned; there was no clicking or clanking, no shot of steam puffing toward the sky.

But isn't that the way life is sometimes? We get this idea in our heads that conjures up exciting images. "The empty nest.

Wow! Won't that be terrific? Certainly by then our furniture will match, our children's rooms will be perfect guest quarters, the garage will no longer be strewn with bikes and skateboard ramps, and we will be wiser women who know who we are."

Unfortunately, that is not always reality. At times the empty nest makes us feel as though we are victims of identity theft. We spent the last half of life so far on a singular project, that of raising children. When we are engaged in any work that requires as much energy and effort as mothering does, we are certain to lose part of ourselves in the process.

Do we feel let down at this crossroads of the empty nest? Did we expect a beautiful exhibit of steam rising with intricate parts turning in a thrilling manner? Should we have "arrived" by now with a career and significant accomplishments, or at least to vicariously enjoy those of our children? Did we expect our children to instantly have promising jobs and perfect marriages that will give us grandchildren when we want them? That would be nice, but at our house, we pine for three unsettled but altruistic artists who ask the big questions of us and of God, which can be unsettling.

Even at our age, some of us still question our own career choices or lack of success. What if I had studied what I really feel gifted to do? Would the full-size rendering of my life look different at this point? One can't help but wonder.

Sometimes I wish I could begin the child-rearing years all over again with the experience and knowledge I have today. But it doesn't work that way. Rather, God grows us and works on our identity *as* we mother our children. He began by carving little "working models" of our lives. He chiseled away on us, creating a new identity more closely aligned to His image.

As it turns out, our little lives have not lost their identity. God is indeed forming us to become who He has in mind for us to be. As we recognize that Christ has been with us all along and is still with us today, our identity is secure in Him. He is the most comprehensive identity theft insurance available for us empty-nest mothers.

It is my prayer that the view from our empty nest will always be upward to our heavenly Father, who lovingly promises to never leave us or forsake us for a moment.

Notes

10. A Love-Hate Relationship with Social Media

1. Ruan Fan "Addicted to 'likes?' Here's how to quit," *Telegraph*, June 14, 2016, http://www.telegraph.co.uk/sponsored/china-watch/society/12211102/social-media-likes-addiction.html.

2. Brent Conrad, "Why Is Facebook Addictive? Twenty-One Reasons for Facebook Addiction," *Tech Addiction*, http://www.techaddiction.ca/why-is-facebook-addictive.html.

3. Madeline L'Engle, *The Irrational Season* (San Francisco, CA: Harper & Row, 1977), 192.

11. Deliver Us from Envy

1. Andrea Shea, "Facebook Envy: How the Social Network Affects Our Self Esteem," *WBUR*, February 20, 2013, http://legacy.wbur.org/2013/02/20/facebook-perfection.

20. The Best Kind of Rest

1. Augustine of Hippo, *Confessions*, ed. Michael P. Foley, tr. F.J. Sheed (Indianapolis, IN: Hackett, 2006), 3.

2. David G. Benner, *Desiring God's Will* (Downers Grove, IL: IVP Books, 2015), 45.

22. The Classics, My Early Morning Friends

1. *The Books of the Bible New Testament* (Colorado Springs, CO: Biblica, 2011).

2. Jeanne Guyon, *Experiencing the Depths of Jesus Christ* (Jacksonville, FL: SeedSowers, 1975), 4.

3. Guyon, *Experiencing the Depths of Jesus Christ.*

4. Richard Foster and James Bryan Smith, *Devotional Classics* (New York, NY: Harper-Collins, 1993), 81.

5. Brother Lawrence, quoted in Parkhurst, *The Believer's Secret to the Abiding Presence* (Minneapolis, MN: Bethany House), 97.

6. Lawrence, quoted in Parkhurst, *The Believer's Secret to the Abiding Presence*, 105.

7. Foster and Smith, *Devotional Classics*, 33-39.

8. John of the Cross, quoted in Foster and Smith, *Devotional Classics*, 36.

9. C.S. Lewis, *Mere Christianity* (New York, NY: Macmillan, 1952), 169.

10. Lewis, *Mere Christianity*, 170.

11. Henri Nouwen, *With Burning Hearts: A Meditation on the Eucharistic Life* (Maryknoll, NY: Orbis Books, 1994).

23. The Boomers and the Boomerangs

1. Andy Kiersz, "Here's how many millennials live with their parents in each US state," *Business Insider*, May 3, 2017, http://www.businessinsider.com/millennials-living-at-home-state-map-2017-5.

2. Richard Fry, "It's becoming more common for young adults to live at home–and for longer stretches," Pew Research Center, May 5, 2017, http://www.pewresearch.org/fact-tank/2017/05/05/its-becoming-more-common-for-young-adults-to-live-at-home-and-for-longer-stretches/.

3. Fry, "It's Becoming More Common."

4. Fry, "It's Becoming More Common."

5. Tim Henderson, "For Millennials, Marriage Can Wait," *Huffington Post*, December 21, 2016, https://www.huffingtonpost.com/entry/for-many-millennials-marriage-can-wait_us_58594a53e4b0630a254235b6.

25. Millennials: What We Learn from Their Thoughts on Things

1. Jura Koncius, "Stuff It: Millennials Nix Their Parents' Treasures," *Washington Post*, March 27, 2015, https://www.washingtonpost.com/local/boomers-unwanted-inheritance/2015/03/27/0e75ff6e-45c4-11e4-b437-1a7368204804_story.html?utm_term=.7b4a88d27d47.

2. Koncius, "Stuff It."

3. Tom Verde, "Aging Parents with Lots of Stuff, and Children Who Don't Want It," *New York Times*, August 18, 2017, https://www.nytimes.com/2017/08/18/your-money/aging-parents-with-lots-of-stuff-and-children-who-dont-want-it.html.

4. Jura Koncius, "Declutter like a Swede: Think about your heirs," *Washington Post*, http://digitaledition.chicagotribune.com/infinity/article_popover_share.aspx?guid=c8e64240-1ea0-47c8-a4b3-d8160a56c476.

26. Apple Pie at Midnight

1. Sara Fishko, "The Fishko Files: Chopin's 'Raindrop' Prelude," *WNYC*, March 18, 2010, http://www.wnyc.org/story/72008-the-fishko-files-chopins-raindrop-prelude/.

29. Saying "I'm Sorry"

1. Madeline L'Engle, *The Irrational Season* (San Francisco, CA: Harper & Row, 1977), 136.

33. Finding Fulfillment in the Emptiness

1. Julian of Norwich, quoted in Richard Foster and James Bryan Smith, *Devotional Classics* (New York, NY: HarperCollins, 1993), 70-71.

37. Writing Down the Empty Nest

1. Thai Nguyen, "10 Surprising Benefits You'll Get from Keeping a Journal," *Huff-Post,* February 13, 2015, https://www.huffingtonpost.com/thai-nguyen/benefits-of-journaling-_b_6648884.html.

38. Because He Bends Down to Listen

1. Julian of Norwich, quoted in Richard Foster and James Bryan Smith, *Devotional Classics* (New York, NY: HarperCollins, 1993), 70.

2. Julian, in Foster and Smith, *Devotional Classics*, 70.

3. Julian, in Foster and Smith, *Devotional Classics*, 71.

4. Julian, in Foster and Smith, *Devotional Classics*, 68.

40. Ground the Helicopter

1. Kate Bayless, "What is Helicopter Parenting?" *Parents*, 2013, http://www.parents.com/parenting/better-parenting/what-is-helicopter-parenting/.

2. Joel L. Young, "The Effect of 'Helicopter Parenting,'" *Psychology Today*, January 25, 2017, https://www.psychologytoday.com/blog/when-your-adult-child-breaks-your-heart/201701/the-effects-helicopter-parenting.

3. Anna Almandrala, "5 Signs You Were Raised by Helicopter Parents," *Huffington Post*, September 30, 2015, https://www.huffingtonpost.com/entry/5-ways-to-tell-you-were-raised-by-helicopter-parents_us_5609de6ee4b0dd850308e260.

4. Young, "The Effect of 'Helicopter Parenting.'"

..n Do Us Part

ᴊusan Bonifant, "The Empty Nest Marriage, Deciding Whether to Stay or Go," *Washington Post*, April 13, 2017, https://www.washingtonpost.com/news/parenting/wp/2017/04/13/the-empty-nest-marriage-deciding-whether-to-stay-or-go/?utm_term=.6dd4e87bfb61.

2. Mark Banschick, "The High Failure Rate of Second and Third Marriages," *Psychology Today*, February 6, 2012, https://www.psychologytoday.com/blog/the-intelligent-divorce/201202/the-high-failure-rate-second-and-third-marriages.